Jim: The Author's Self-Centered Memoir on the Great Jim Brown
James Toback

Genius of the heart: as it is possessed by that great Hidden One...
whose voice can climb into the underworld of any psyche, who
never speaks a word or looks a look in which there is not some
hindsight, some complexity of allure, whose craftsmanship
includes knowing how to be an illusion—not an illusion of
what he is, but of what constitutes one more compulsion upon
his followers to follow him ever more immediately and
thoroughly—*genius of the heart*, which renders dumb all that
is loud and complaisant, teaching it how to listen, which
smooths rough souls and creates a taste in them for a new
desire...*Genius of the heart*, upon whose touch everyone departs
richer, not full of grace, not surprised, not enriched and
oppressed as though by strange goods, but richer in himself,
newer than before, cracked wide open...

Nietzsche
Beyond Good and Evil

Contents

Introduction

Thirty-seven years ago the author of Jim, twenty-seven at the time, sported tight jeans with a waist of 30 inches and length of 32. Today the length is still 32. The waist has experienced alterations significant enough to be labeled radical. I serve up this tidbit of news concerning external shift not so much in the service of perverse self-mockery as in metaphor for the dimensions—vast and diverse—of change experienced internally since my days of cohabitation with Jim Brown, described and analyzed in the work that these brief words are intended to introduce.

I was hesitant at first to accept the invitation of Brett Ratner (whose generosity and initiative in starting this new and elegantly packaged imprint are commendable beyond measure) to write an introduction at all. The notion seemed to smack of apology—or even disclaimer. But when I actually read my own text—which I had not done since proofreading the original galleys, I had the ferociously complicated response of a father reunited with a son to whom he had been inordinately close after a separation of nearly three decades. "Oh how wonderful it is to see you again," I felt like crying out after ten pages—a rich congeries of admiration (of the great energy, boldness, and disdain of danger), envy (of the array of literary allusions and quotations at his fingertips, the unlimited and relaxed sexual confidence, the full head of thick hair, the extraordinary basketball and tennis skills), and wincing embarrassment (at the barely concealed need to show off, to impress, to distinguish himself from the rest of the entire white male population—at least in America—in his unique ability to be thought of as "one of us" in an all-star, all-black world).

What a longing to be that person again!—with the provision that the artistic achievements, sufferings, acquaintance with death, cynical wisdom, romantic love, and joy of fatherhood could all be incorporated into the mix. What longing to be that person again—for a week or two at least, with an option to renew.

James Toback
December 2008
New York City

An Early Memory

I used to play in Central Park, shooting silver six guns, rolls of caps stuffed in my pockets, ready to reload as soon as I ran out; would shoot at little girls, gleeful at the fear I could so easily induce; at boys passing by, many of them older and bigger, at couples in love, strolling; at anyone. I could not have been more than six, but I was cocky, unafraid.

At school, I was the leader of a gang of two, the other being Barry, and together we ruled the grade. There were other gangs; but I was tall for my age, Barry was big and determined, and we always seemed to prevail. Each day, school let out, our mothers would take us to the park, where we would climb trees, slide down rocks, wrestle in the grass, sharpen our shooting eyes.

One day Barry's mother picked us up, said that my mother would meet us later at the park's Mall, would bring Julia's nephews to play, too. Julia was our cook, the only Negro I knew.

Barry and I played that day as always, laughing, running, wrestling, killing. I was lodged in a tree, having forgotten my mother, when I looked down, saw her coming over. Following just behind, two boys, one taller than I, the other smaller, both thin, both black; white t-shirts and dark pants. I watched my mother introduce them to Barry's, saw them shake her hand, stare at the ground. Barry, nearby, went over and said hello. I waited in the tree.

"Jim! Come down."

She walked over to the tree, stood below looking up.

"Come down and say hello to Thomas and Eugene."

"No." I had decided to remain up there until the intruders were gone.

"They're Julia's nephews!" she said, her voice a loud whisper, "they're very nice boys. They came all the way out here to meet you."

"I don't want to meet them."

She walked back to the bench. Barry lent the tall boy his gun and I watched him shoot. He did it the way Lash Larue and the Cisco Kid did, whipping his left hand across the hammer rapidly,

3

knees bent, right hand holding the gun perfectly still. Barry and the small boy raced from the bench to the bust of Robert Burns, about fifty yards away, the small boy winning by yards. The tall boy kept shooting.

"You outta caps!" he yelled to Barry.

It didn't sound right. Not "You outta caps"; you said, "You're out of caps."

I jumped down from the tree, one long plunge. Ordinarily, I would have edged out from branch to branch, but I wanted the tall boy to see my risk. I landed hard and hurt my knee, but I got up quickly, turned my back so he wouldn't see the pain.

"I'm Thomas," putting out his hand. I turned and shook it.

"You got caps? I run outta caps."

I gave him a roll. His hair was short; he had wide, beautiful dark eyes, big lips, thin skin. Black shoes, the kind I'd always wanted; mine were a dull brown.

"Can you do this?"

I drew my gun from my holster, whirled it around my index finger several times, tossed it in the air, caught it on my finger, whirled it again, fired. Thomas laughed hysterically.

"That's good! Whoo-ee!"

"Can you do it?"

"Haw, I never tried it."

"Try it."

He tried it with Barry's gun and twirled it well, but when he tossed it in the air, it came down badly and he caught it at the end.

"You couldn't do it."

"Yeah, but I bet I could beat you at a foot race."

"Bet you couldn't."

Barry and Eugene were coming over and heard.

"I wanna race, too," Eugene said.

"I'm too tired," Barry said.

"Come on, just to the statue," I said.

"No, you guys race," Barry said. "I'll say go."

Suddenly, I felt helpless; I did not want to lose but knew I was going to.

"On your mark, get set, go!"

I had jumped the gun, but no one called it so I just kept tearing ahead, grunting. Halfway, looked back. Eugene was five feet behind but Thomas was almost with me, strides long, bouncing high, feet quick and light. Ten yards from the end, he passed me, was pulling away when he reached the statue.

"How old are you?" I said.

"Nine years old."

"When I'm nine, I'll beat you."

"When you're nine, I won't be nine no more."

On the way home our mothers walked ahead, then Barry and I, behind us Thomas and Eugene. I felt funny.

"Do you like Thomas and Eugene?"

"No," I said. "I hate them."

I turned around, waited for Thomas to catch up. When he did, I pulled out my gun, gripped it at the end, swung hard, cracked him on the skull with the handle. He fell to the ground, groaning, then screaming, tears in his eyes.

"What happened!" My mother rushed back.

"I didn't mean it!" Eugene was on his knees, holding Thomas. I knew they wouldn't hurt me and I wasn't afraid of my mother's rage; but I was trembling.

"Please, Thomas, forgive me; I'm sorry." I got down on the ground, gripped his hand tight. "Don't be hurt. I want to be your friend."

Apology

Early in December 1968, I flew from New York to Los Angeles to meet Jim Brown and to write about him. I had watched him on television and, whenever possible, in person, on fall and winter Sundays—melding force, speed, cunning, and grace, each week reestablishing himself as the most magnificent running back, perhaps the greatest football player at any position, who ever lived. Football had displaced baseball as the leading national sport. Boys of eight and nine in Topeka, Boise, Memphis, Buffalo, and San Francisco now dreamed of becoming Brown or Lance Rentzel or Gale Sayers; boys whose fathers thirty-five years earlier had imagined themselves Babe Ruth, Ty Cobb, or Christy Mathewson. Construction workers, call girls, politicians, actors, students, stockbrokers talked about the Jets and the Raiders, the Chiefs, Lions, Chargers, and Browns, with authentic enthusiasm; rarely exhibiting more than moderate interest in the other sports filling the American year. Baseball had become slow and dull except at the end of a season in a tight pennant race or World Series. Basketball was fast, but promised more than it finally yielded, legally repressing the violence it suggested at every turn. Hockey was chaotic and boxing so polluted even bookmakers recoiled. Only football constituted a full and satisfactory transformation of energy.

In an essay on football as the most intellectual sport, the intellectual's "secret vice," William Phillips, a literary critic by profession, discovers its ultimate appeal in its unique ability to validate the most primitive feelings about violence, patriotism, and manhood:

The similarity to war is unmistakable: each game is a battle with its own game-plan, each season a campaign, the whole thing a series of wars. Football strategy is like military strategy;

the different positions, each with its own functions but coordinated with the rest of the team, are like the various branches of the armed services. There is even a general draft. And one is loyal to one's country—according to geography and the accident of birth. There is also a parallel to Vietnam, in the support of teams in foreign cities by local fans, which is considered as a hang-up, if not treason. For intellectuals, particularly—but also for a growing number of people generally—these are feelings they would ordinarily feel ashamed of; so pro ball legitimizes their untamed feelings the way *Evergreen* accommodates voyeurs. All sports serve as some kind of release, but the rhythm of football is geared particularly to the violence and the peculiar combination of order and disorder of modern life.

It was Jim Brown who, during the decade from 1957 to 1965, had done more than any other man to originate what became a national obsession with the game. He was a consistent and spectacular warrior, the embodiment of his team, a crystallization of physical potency. More, he introduced a new dimension to the sport, as its first black hero.

It is in this last role that Brown opened his possibilities for the future. He had invaded the American imagination, black and white, with a thrust only rare figures in a generation achieve. When he shifted gears and became, in less than a year, a movie star, the potential of his influence erased limitation. If there were a black boy anywhere in America whose vision of manhood excluded both sports and entertainment, he was a freak, a mutation of consciousness. Apart from serving as channels of style for stored rage, such endeavors provided the cleanest entrance into the American dream of independence, power, wealth, and fame, the promise almost exclusively of whites before the sixties. What that dream became in the life of Jim Brown would hold large interest for young blacks. His form of life, relation to both races, feelings about America, satisfaction or frustration with his own role, would suggest much about the nature of the dream, whether it was worth pursuing or whether—as white Americans had long been discovering—its achievement, at best, solved no significant problems and, at worst, compounded original dilemmas.

So by coming to know Brown and, finally, by writing about him, one could hope to approach and to understand certain mysteries in America, as well as to measure one of her largest and darkest heros. The question of race had become the most complicated and serious force in national life. Everyone had an opinion about "the blacks," everyone speculated on what "they" wanted, what they had been and were, how white people could or couldn't live with them in the future. Books on the subject—novels, plays, sociological treatises, historical studies—were emitted from writers of both races. If Jim Brown were no more the Black Man than Roy Innis or Miles Davis (or Bob Teague), he was involved in more black worlds than any other single Negro. Apart from sports and movies, he was the founder and president of the Black Economic Union and in frequent touch with black political, cultural, and economic leaders all over the country.

There was more, however, to my interest in Brown, to the intuition that he was important beyond himself—to America—and that I would be able to answer questions about myself if I could come to understand something of him. In 1966 David Susskind was taping a television interview with Martin Luther King. During a lengthy analysis of the causes of racial tension in America, King discussed history, social structure, religion, economics, cultural roots, and political philosophy. When Susskind called for a commercial, King told him: "You know, all this is important, but it avoids the central issue, which, of course, is sex." The revelation itself was not so astonishing as the context in which it was placed. That it should have come as an aside confined to the privacy of a station break is typical of the insistence of nearly all analysts of American racial matters on evading the seminal point in public forum—this insistence despite its unprecedentedly easy accessibility. By reputation at least, which alone informed my impression of him at the time, Jim Brown was without peer in affording insight into that issue; lurid tales of freak scenes, brutality, an ineluctable erotic flow.

Since the age of six, when I had met Thomas in Central Park, my concern with cap pistols and the refinements of wielding and firing them had shifted into an obsession with other guns, not revolvers but juice shooters, and time with Brown promised recognitions of what my own powers and motivations were. So I landed in Los Angeles in a condition of great excitement and anticipation; tempered, however, by a vague sense of uneasiness, something close to fear.

First Encounter

That first morning, I spent an inordinate amount of time getting ready—shaved twice, showered, washed my hair, combed it three ways before decided on a style, dressed in black bell pants, a white ruffled shirt, and a purple velvet coat. As I waited in front of the Beverly Hills Hotel for Brown's agent, Paul Block, to pick me up, it occurred to me that even a first engagement with a lovely girl rarely had engendered a religious attention of quite such absurdly vain proportions.

Block pulled up in a blue Thunderbird. He was in his late twenties, but he was soft; blond and large, nervous. In four years he had become one of the most successful agents in Hollywood. Sitting next to him in the front seat, I decided that he would be lucky to live another five years.

"You better watch out," I said. "You're going to cop a heart attack."

"It's the only way to live," he said. "I'm on the move twenty-four hours a day. That's Hollywood. If you dig the people you're working for, you go all out. And I'll tell you something: of all my clients—and I've got Sharon Tate and Trini Lopez and Eddie Fisher—Jim's the greatest. People give you this bullshit about his being mean and hating whites, but he relates to everyone on an honest, personal level. If he likes you, there isn't a thing he won't tell you or do for you, and that goes if you're green or pink or whatever."

It wasn't particularly hot, but Bloch was sweating madly.

"Now this is for Esquire you're writing?"

"They sent me here."

Indeed, they had. And the reminder shot an uncomfortable shiver through my stomach. Esquire had become a literate fusion of Mad, Vogue, and Confidential and was unlikely to be happy with less than the portrait of a malicious monkey, hungry to devour white bananas; and suddenly I knew that the article would never appear, for I was certain I was going to like Jim Brown.

"Everyone wants a story about Jim. He's the hottest property in Hollywood. He'll be making a million dollars a picture in a couple of years. But let me warn you of one thing. If he doesn't like you, he'll clam up. He won't say a word. He'll just wait for you to leave. He doesn't pander to anyone."

I liked Bloch for that. Not many press agents would have entertained, let alone offered, so dangerous a notion of their "property."

Brown lives high in the hills over Sunset Strip. We descended a long driveway, pulled up on a large asphalt basketball court in front of the house.

"He's yours. Ring the bell."

I got out and Bloch waved, driving away. I looked up at the basket on the garage wall, pumped in three imaginary jump shots. Loose, I walked to the door, knocked. Brown opened, two inches taller than I, the beginnings of a beard, dressed in a red sweatshirt, black jeans cut off just above the knee, high white sneakers. He was big, if not so imposingly large as I had imagined. The bones of his face were strong but angled well, eyes slanted, Indian, skin deep tan and thick, with light bumps off the jaw, hair black and soft and neat. His nose was close to flat, broad; the lips tight, curved. A smart, hard face. He looked me up and down quickly, then stared into my eyes. I stared back for several counts, then disappointed myself by turning away to look again at the basket. I sensed, fancifully perhaps, that Brown had already made up his mind about me, that whatever passed between us now or in the future, nothing would radically alter the impression; and I was uneasy, far away myself from the possibility of realizing a similarly quick sense of him. I looked back and he was still staring.

"That's my sport," I said.

"You're much too pretty for basketball."

I stuck out my hand, palm up. He slapped it, then flipped over and I slapped his in turn. Not the openers of a Jewish intellectual from New York, and I was happy about it. "I still want to take you on."

"I dig," said Brown, and then laughed. It was the most remarkable laugh I had ever heard, a low, rhythmic chuckle, vibrating from his chest up through his neck, into his mouth, and finally out his nose, almost a sneer there, immediately contradicted by a light, high whee of delight. A subtle and wonderfully complicated laugh, sounding pleasure at his own remark, at my simple determination, and at a thousand secret jokes in the past, no few of them bitter, which he had never shared with anyone and never would.

" 'Laughter is not at all a bad beginning for a friendship, and it is by far the best ending for one,'" I said.

"Who said that?" Brown asked out of the corner of his eyes.

"I did." I held my face straight for a second; then smiled and added, "Oscar Wilde. How did you know I didn't?"

"That ain't your voice. You've got a lot of voices, but that's not one of them."

He led me into a bright living room, long yellow-and-white sofa, lamps, a tan stereo console, marble table, a glass wall looking out on a pool; below, on Los Angeles, the mountains, and the sea. We sat down.

"Listen, I hate interviews, but I'm never going to get a thing for this article if I don't do it directly, so let me run down my preconceptions, and you check me if you don't agree."

"Okay."

"Start with a premise. There are all sorts of distinctions one can make about people, but the essential one is the distinction between the artist and the non-artist. The artist is interested in the moment, in arresting time with the creation of a striking form, with his body, his mind, his words. He's not concerned with the functional, only with the grace and rhythm and harmony of his effort. And it will show across the board: in the way he moves, works, talks, drives, fights, makes love. You're the only real artist football has produced, which is why people would rather see you run for five yards than Matt Snell for fifty. Sayers and Simpson might be as effective, but they, and no one else, give the sense of unity with time and space that you do. Just as Stan Musial was as *good* as Ted Williams, but also nowhere near him, because he was never an artist and Williams always was; or Joe Louis and Ali, the same thing. Or Eugene Ormandy and Leonard Bernstein. People even love bandits and killers if they're artists, which is what sold *Bonnie and Clyde.*"

I stopped; wondered, suddenly, if my assessment of Brown wasn't fantasy, whether he wasn't simply amused by a magazine writer telling him, after five minutes of acquaintance, who he was.

"Look, I'm digging everything you're saying, but we can talk later, because that's not what you want to do now and it's not what I want to do."

"Where's your ball?"

He pointed to the hall; I followed him outside onto

13

the court. I had seen him fifteen years before in Madison Square Garden, a marvelous forward for Syracuse, playing evenly with Tommy Heinsohn, later to become one of the finest scorers and rebounders in the professional ranks. I had made a fair mark in high school and played intramural ball at Harvard, but my credentials were hardly of the same class. I had a good jump shot from the corner and from twenty-five feet straight away but had never won a coach's heart with aggressiveness off the boards or sharp defensive moves. Still, I was not without confidence that I could take Brown one on one. I wanted badly to win and was by nature enough of a gambler to believe there was a hidden, direct proportion between the intensity of my desire for victory and the chances of achieving it. Also, the supreme casualness of Brown's movements, something close to somnambulance in his gait now, opened a vision to me, a quick, sweet flash of ten hard, line jump shots, poured consecutively, shutting out, dazzling Jim Brown.

"Go," he said, flipping me the ball.

I stood twenty feet away, he giving room. I bounced the ball once, felt the seam, the hard rubber firm on my fingertips; jumped straight up, drove the ball low and true, swish, through the nets. He retrieved the ball, tossed it back, waited, midway between the board and me. I bounced again, leaped, this time arched the ball slightly, softly through. I felt my rhythm, knew I couldn't lose; would decorate—baroque, lovely variations on the way to my win. I moved to my left on a low dribble, cut right, stopped, turned at the peak of my jump, threw the ball through the hoop.

Brown smiled. "Nice!" He still hadn't moved. It suddenly occurred to me that he wasn't aware the game had started, that he was simply watching me warm up.

"Three nothing," I said for reassurance.

He nodded.

I drove hard to the right corner, passing him, immobile, pushed a high, delicate shot, fading away. "Naulls!" I yelled as the ball swished through. Brown laughed his laugh.

"Was he your favorite?"

"One of them," I said. "Four nothing."

I put in another jump shot from the out-of-bounds line, he still passive.

"What are you doing?" I said.

"Watching you.

"I'm gonna shut you out," I said. I was Muhammad Ali. The game was an out bet.

He grinned.

I scored three more, then checked: "Ten game, right?" He nodded.

"Well, here's nine," sending a long one-hander cleanly through. "Cousy!" I bellowed.

Brown picked up the ball, moved slowly at me, stopping finally no more than two inches away; looked into my eyes.

"You really think you're gonna win?" His voice was soft, a whisper.

"That's right."

"You *really* do!" voice still quiet, but with an edge now, challenging.

"I couldn't lose if I tried."

Brown smiled. One didn't need to be a student of the psychology of language to infer from the construction the will to submission it had unwittingly revealed.

"Come on," I said, almost angrily.

"You ready?" He laughed.

Crowded, I tried to drive around him, but he reached

in and slapped the ball off the dribble in the direction of the basket, sprang on it, and in the same motion, glided up over the rim and stuffed it.

"Nine one," he said, serious.

"Cocksucker," I said, but then couldn't help laughing with him.

"Ready?"

I nodded, and he threw in a soft twenty-foot jump shot. On the next three plays, I went for steals off his dribble, missing as he drove by for layups. Two long hook shots, one from the foul line, one from the corner (followed by a cry of "Heinsohn!") cut the deficit to two. He winked as he took the ball out. Facing me, bouncing the ball dangerously high, almost to his neck, he said, "Take it away. I'm giving it to you."

I started to lunge, then hesitated, but it was too late. He was off and around me, up over the rim, ramming for nine eight.

"You'll never get away with that again."

"You sure?"

"Yeah."

"You as sure about that as you were that you were going to win this game?"

"Right. Don't worry; I'll still win."

"The motherfucker sure is *determined*," Brown said. "Got to give him credit for that."

He moved into his slow, high dribble again, left hand leading him to his left, right hand to his right, tracing and retracing an arc of a hundred degrees twenty feet away from the basket. Playing loose defense, keying to his rhythm, I waited. Suddenly, as he was switching hands on his dribble, I swung my right arm down and in, hand touching, controlling the ball, guiding it away, mine now, a clean steal. I moved in, open, stopped five feet away, leaped high, pumped, and shot the ball—long, comically long, far beyond the basket, off the far end of the backboard, from which it skipped out of bounds. I felt a twist of nausea—dry, foul taste in my mouth; threw a right hand lead into the wooden garage door. I was twelve years old again, hurling my racket in disgust during the finals of a Florida Boys Tennis Tournament.

"Nate Bowman," I said quietly.

"Ready?"

I watched him float two push shots through the net, ending the game.

"See, I'm supposed to be an animal," Brown said as we went back into the house, "a big, bad, evil spook who can't think and can't talk. I'm supposed to rely on my size and strength. But, really, that's bullshit, first of all, it's too easy to do that, and secondly, it's deceptive, because it doesn't work. All real victories are psychological."

" 'O, it is excellent

To have a giant's strength; but it is tyrannous

To use it like a giant.'"

"That's not you, either. Shakespeare?"

"*Measure for Measure.*"

We moved into the kitchen and Brown took out two large bottles of orange juice, offering one to me. Gluttonously, next to the sink, we drank.

"See, what really intrigues me is finding out the rules and the structure of a game, whatever kind it is, then playing, working, and winning within it. Why do you think Russell always beat Chamberlain? He whipped him mentally. He outmuscled his mind. I like to win, and since you can do just so many things with your time, I only get into games I like and can do well with."

"I know what you mean. I don't ski, for instance."

Brown laughed and I felt good; it was the sort of humor I usually appreciate without company. I watched the end of his smile, saw that that was where you could see what the laugh meant. This time it froze abruptly and he looked hard.

"This all extends into relationships with people, you know. I mean, if I'm interested in someone, I'll spend time with him—work, play, whatever. But if I'm not, I don't have time for no amenities. I don't rap if I have nothing to say to someone. I just walk away. And if a cat or a chick's rappin' to me and don't have nothin' to say, I'll turn them right out."

It was not impossible that he had said exactly the same words, with the same hard look, following the same laugh, to a candidate for the Gaylords, a formidable gang on the South Shore of Long Island which he had ruled as warlord twenty years before. In an autobiography written with Myron Cope in 1964, he included an anecdote that suggests the stance he had to assume in that role.

Our boys carried switchblade penknives but only to build up their own egos. They liked to stand on street corners clicking their knives, but they never used them in fights. Fights generally wound up with warlord pitted against warlord, with everyone else forming a circle.

As warlord of the Gaylords, I rarely had to fight, simply because my opponents almost always backed down. Since my first year on Long Island—the year I'd fought my way to the top of the class—I'd had a fairly strong reputation. Still, I should have known that sooner or later I'd have to face a blade. One night in Hempstead I did.

We had invited ourselves to a party being held by a rival gang. For a while, all was peaceful. I was just standing there, listening to the phonograph music and minding my own business. The rival warlord, however, had been drinking liquor and growing belligerent on it. He swayed with the music and snapped his fingers; then, pretending to be only releasing his feelings for the music, gave me a hard slap on the back. I knew he meant it as a challenge. I said nothing. He slapped me a second time, and I told him, "Look, don't slap me on the back." I moved a few steps away. "Oh, you think you're something big?" he said. "You guys come in here in your sharp jackets and think you're something." I said to myself, "Here it goes." I told him, "Look, we can settle this fast. Just come outside." He got loud. "Sure I'll come outside," he shouted for everyone to hear. "I'll wipe up the street with you." We went outside, and everyone crowded around us. Then, click! Out came his blade.

I had no knife myself. I never carried one, because I never believed a knife would make me any bigger and I knew I could never cut anyone. Now I had to think fast. I reached into my pocket and held my hand there for a menacing moment. All I had in it was a ringful of keys. With a great show of purpose, I worked one key into position so that it pointed sharply against my trousers. Then I slipped my hand from my pocket. The instant I did, my opponent closed his knife and shoved it into his pocket. He smiled weakly. I opened the palm of my hand, revealing a fistful of keys, and then hauled and gave him a hard slap in the face. "Let's go home," I said to the Gaylords.

His words had now stirred in me simultaneously the awe, confidence, and fear that any good warlord will induce either in one he seeks to lead or in one he looks to fight. But why stop with street gangs and the domain of a city block? It was no less than the qualities that the ruler of a nation, of nations, must evoke; the mark of a dictator, benevolent to those he loves, lethal to any who might betray him, that Jim Brown was making on my mind.

"You sound like a leader."

"I have my organization."

It was a difficult line to put over, but he had made a good shot at it. From a motel-chain operator or an automobile manufacturer it would have sounded pompous, perhaps even from Floyd McKissick or Rhody McCoy. But Brown had said it softly, firmly, and with a suggestion of embarrassment, self-depreciation, a hint that next to the hope that it would become an important organization was the fear, even the recognition, that it would not.

"I'll have Kenny run you down there tomorrow. But briefly, this is what we're trying to do." He sat down at the kitchen table, leaning forward, a voice fuller now, keyed to a lower pitch, words more distinct. He was about to make a presentation in front of a representative from the Ford Foundation. No double negatives here.

"What I'm interested in is Green Power—money. You can't begin to talk about equality or integration until you've given black people the opportunity to make good bread and to run things, to learn about what they can and can't do. What we need is to own businesses, to do the hiring and firing, not just the applying. We have to get black people participating en masse in the American economy, and the major step in this direction is establishing them as *producers* as well as consumers. They have to create a market of products for consumers, both black and white, that will compete with—and thereby actually help—the white market. There are precedents for this, too. In the South, for example, where the desperation has been the greatest, black-run businesses have made their biggest success: Atlanta Life, North Carolina Mutual."

His face was a mask, the eyes looking into space beyond me, the mouth moving evenly, mechanically. He had shifted gears; he was miles away from himself, white.

"What's it called?"

"The Black Economic Union. It used to be the Negro Industrial and Economic Union, but I changed it because I had to spend too much time explaining why I sanctioned the word Negro. Personally, it doesn't matter to me one way or another. Black, Negro, spook, blood, spade, boo-boo: what the fuck! You know?"

He laughed, back now to his own rhythm. Then he cut it off and returned to the conference room, fund raising. "Let me run down the background to you. In '63 the situation was neat. There were relatively few organizations, and each had specific goals which were pretty clearly defined. Groups like King's and the old SNCC were after equality with integration; the Muslims wanted equality, but in a segregated system. All of it was nonviolent. Today, you've got a whole spectrum of approaches. First, there are the conservatives: apolitical cats like the late Sonny Liston, who was looking to make a good living for himself but couldn't have cared less what happened to other black cats. Or politically oriented people like Roy Wilkins, who are looking to improve things politely and quietly. Economically oriented cats like Whitney Young, who try to get jobs for spooks in white industry, and philosophers like Bayard Rustin, who also want integration but talk about self-improvement where integration isn't feasible.

"At the other end you've got the radical cats, the Garveyans, who talk about Africa as the black cat's real home and want to set up a black state in America. And the Movement, which talks violence and sometimes acts it:

Stokely and Rap Brown and Karenga, who aren't interested in working with white people at all, and the Panthers, who are. So the debate over all this really centers around a few central questions: integration or segregation, America or Africa, capitalism or what Cleaver calls 'Yankee Doodle Dandy Socialism.'"

Brown's eyes came down on me, through me. His hands, massive and scarred from cleat cuts, opened in front of him, then traveled up to his hair, drove through it, dropped on his lap. His mouth thinned, curling down at the corner. I felt a sense of deadness, heavy boredom. I imagined he would have given much at that moment to be out playing. I knew, at any rate, that I would.

"The BEU fits in somewhere between these two extremes. It assumes that capitalism can still work, that you have to be self-sufficient economically before you can talk realistically about intangibles like equality and spiritual recognition, and that these ends can be achieved best by establishing black-controlled and black-oriented economic entities."

He looked up, over at me, at the wall; repeating, rehearsing, recording.

"Integration is natural and desirable. All a black cat has to do is look and he'll find plenty of hip young white people, and that's beautiful. But no spook with his balls is gonna grovel. I don't have to convince nobody that I'm as good as he is; and I don't have to try to get no one to accept me."

His voice had hardened, and his face was tight and mean. I noticed that he looked his best this way: steely, brave, intelligent, unyielding. Then he softened, voice relaxed, eyes wandering.

"If a heavy white cat wants to swing with a heavy black

cat, that's cool. But the black cat ain't gonna beg for it, cause he's got his own thing going."

"What about Africa? That wouldn't fit in with your organization very well."

"Look, an American black cat, no matter what he may want to think or want you to think, is more American than African. His roots are in Cleveland or L.A. or New York, not in Mali or Timbuktu. He digs cars and records and sports and movies and air conditioners, and he ain't about to give them up for voodoo. I'm working within the system. The motto of the organization is Produce, Achieve, and Prosper."

It was hardly a revolutionary program. It suggested pursuits already encouraged by Floyd McKissick and Roy Innis and a dozen other black organizers in cities all over America. But it had a unique advantage: precisely the leadership of Brown. If a young Negro were thinking of money, how to make it in his future, Brown's success, his mystique, would have to excite interest in his particular group. And if a young Negro weren't happy about the idea of working within the system, he would be more likely to reconsider, upon learning that Brown—as distinguished from McKissick, Innis, Young, etc.—was.

Still, I was finding it increasingly difficult to listen. Flashbacks of the basketball game—especially the recurring image of my errant layup that would have won it for me—interrupted, taunted, and discomforted. And I couldn't take my eyes off his shoulders and arms. The longer I watched him, the larger, the more powerful he became. Such strength, so bald to any observer, would relieve him of all difficulty in emphasizing grace and rhythm, wit, spirit and speed, at the expense of force. This apprehension of that strength, the fine edge of his voice, his darkness, suddenly worked to make me feel uneasy. But it passed, and I pushed myself to hear him.

"There are a number of subsidiary groups, too. The United Athletic Association, for instance, is the first organization to represent athletes negotiating contracts, and to help them in planning investments, endorsements, personal appearances, and off-season employment. In a weird sense, athletes are an exploited class, bought, sold, and traded whenever their owners care to. People tend to think just in terms of the big yearly salaries they read about in the papers. But in fact, the owners just use them as long as they can and then, as a rule, don't give a shit what happens. And this is especially true of black athletes. When I quit, people said I was ungrateful, and the thinking behind it went like this: Here's this big, dumb animal, this nigger, who couldn't have done shit with his life if it hadn't been for football, and now that he's made all that bread, he walks out. He should play himself off the top, into the ground, till he can't run anymore, and then get cut like the bum he really is. Well, fuck that. I didn't owe them nothin'. They paid me to play, to entertain, to put on a show; and I gave my best while I was taking their bread. But an athlete has the right to stop whenever he feels it's best for him to do so. In my case, I got a movie offer and told Art Modell that I was going to take it and that the shooting schedule involved missing part of the training season. He sent word to me in Europe while I was shooting that if I didn't come back right away, I shouldn't bother coming back at all. So I didn't. I quit."

He picked up the basketball and flipped it to me. We passed it back and forth in the kitchen.

"Anyway," he said, rolling it on his arm, "all that's beside the point. The BEU does much more than just work with athletes. We help all kinds of black-run businesses, with loans, recruitments, assistance in training programs, planning."

"Where do whites fit into this?" I asked. Immediately, I regretted the question. I felt like a reporter again, and worse, a bad one, who was missing the point—which I wasn't.

"Any white person who wants to help is more than welcome. I've got some of my friends—Steve McQueen, Lee Marvin, Ernie Borgnine—very interested. And once we get enough black athletes in our fold, we'll start looking to represent whites." He smiled. "Maybe you'll want to join."

"Consider it wanted," I said. "But I'm still going to beat you in basketball."

The Breakup of a Marriage;
Parting and Reunion

Brown had suddenly to go to London, and I left L.A. the next day for New York—home and my wife. I had been married less than a year, but I was restive, away whenever I had the chance, hiding when we were together. How, indeed, could a journey to L.A., time with Brown, longing for a return to release and abandon, intrigue with new forms of sexuality and power, have occurred to me, tempted me, if I hadn't felt bound, encased by my wife? Only self-deception of major proportions would have permitted me to settle on the Esquire assignment as an adequate explanation.

Even frequent trips to Jamaica had served only to corroborate the sense of entrapment. So it was an uneasy time, happy hours over many months regularly marred by suspicion and bitterness on her part, evasion and remorse on mine.

She was a lovely girl by any measure, a delicate, generous, beautiful spirit with a quick, warm wit and a wonderful tolerance for the curiosities and eccentricities of anyone who had shown her the barest kindness. But I had come to the union from impulses and needs far too complex to permit a simple and complementary response to her qualities. She was the granddaughter of the Duke of Marlborough, a grandniece of Winston Churchill, and so had taken on vast symbolic dimensions for me long before I came to know her. How could I rest content with a Cindy Schneider or an Elizabeth Gold (or even with a Linda Camillo, an Ulla Petersen, an Aloise Jeannin) when there was a Consuelo Sarah Churchill (Mimi) Russell to be fought for, won, held, possessed? How? How, given ancestors wandering Hebraically, only three generations back, in Lithuania? How, given thoroughly righteous training and direction, a code structured on the values of industry, denial, safety, and stability? How, when, flipped, the obverse promised Blenheim and three centuries of aristocratic tradition and a world that, historically, had flouted restraint and lived by leisure, indulgence, risk, and fluidity? How, given Harvard, where though my closest friends were Phil Ardery and Barry Custer, Steve Saltonstall and James Thackara, the Spee, the Porcellian and the Delphic would remain closed, hiding those happy, light-eyed boys who assumed with inherited complacence that the lovely girls of the Main Line and Beacon Hill and Hobe Sound were theirs alone, too good, too white, too blue for you, O funny, too-hip freaky Jew? How, finally, given that I had not yet earned a sufficiently strong sense of my own powers and self, a force sure enough to provide certainty that I could hold my place with anyone, that, ultimately, I didn't even need to try, that my own heritage could stand alone? I couldn't; not then, not yet. And I didn't.

With motives so tortuous, the odds on the marriage's working well, lasting any considerable time, were slender indeed. The ceremony itself, the public issue, became at once the metaphorical resolution of my doubts and my quest, and a resounding confutation to all who had dared to suggest, directly or by implication, that there was any situation beyond reach, any fantasy beyond realization. Indeed, the wedding had not been over an hour when, driving to the New York Hilton for the first sanctified night, I began to feel sick and hollow; restricted, tied.

By having convinced *Esquire* to send me to Los Angeles to meet Brown, I had made a choice whose symbolic import could hardly have deluded either Mimi or me. One world, apparently the most distant and exotic I could have found, had now been penetrated and so had to be replaced by another, even more difficult, farther out of reach. And it was, finally, the world I had been seeking all along, for what had been my appeal to the scion of so venerable a British house if not that of the stranger? A compromise; for the true stranger, the true sexual outlaw and source of power in America was not the Jew but, once more removed, the boo. In a significant sense, then, I had been posing all along, posing as a spook, the personification of whose world I had now gone to face and, by earning, to join.

Two days into the return to New York, and Mimi was gone. Without a word. In the end, a tough girl. Had wanted only love, attention, time: a husband; when she had to believe, finally, that it was not dependably there, that I wasn't he, she left. But it was precisely that tough-ness—the knowledge that despite the warmth, loyalty, and kindness she had been so eager to give, I would have to be good, my best, with her—that had drawn me to her originally. However our decent and warm moments may have been obfuscated by the mythology I had constructed, they had survived as memory; and now, concomitant to her departure, they sharpened, haunting. The presence of her absence was everywhere. I was in love, but this time alone.

The next week was empty, desperate. I was hungry, but couldn't eat; exhausted to the point of vertigo, but couldn't sleep (except in short fits, dreams of her body in my arms, ruthlessly ended by awakening in darkness without her). I was restless but couldn't coordinate, even move. I went to the movies but couldn't follow plots, remember the titles; danced, my rhythm bollixed, my time wrong; walked marathon miles around the furniture of our living room; talked with commiserating friends whose faces were suddenly strange, voices empty and flat.

I was convinced I wanted her back; that if only she were to return I would, at last, be satisfied, need no more adventure, no new places, people, approaches, risks. But she wouldn't come or even talk to me, and I stayed at home, waiting.

Abruptly, there was an interruption. Brown called from London, said he just wanted to check me out. First astonished, then exhilarated, I laid control aside, told him my wife was gone and that I felt terrible. He was quiet, then said it was too bad, a sad story. A minute later, he had to go. I was angry at the timing, the cut-off too sudden, lacking, what? Sympathy? Not at all what I wanted. Rather: once past the surprise and elation at his call, I understood that, absurdly, I had somehow *expected* it, had, moreover, somehow assumed he would come, come across the sea, Jim Dandy to the *rescue*, to get her back for me, to tell her, make her feel, you don't know what you've done and what you've lost; he's as good as I am, but he's *white*, see, the only one, an animal, but a Harvard animal, who knows Charles d'Orléans and Yeats; you can't say no, crazy girl. Take him back. Today. But he wasn't coming. He had called but heard things were bad and so was through.

The next morning I was pacing, chain-smoking, when the bell rang, and there, six two and two twenty, was J.B.

"You want some fresh orange juice?"

Again, the incredible enacted, I instinctively accepted it as an inevitability all along.

"Yeah, that would be good."

"Long trip?"

"Yeah."

"You sleep?"

"No, not really."

"Neither did I."

I felt at that moment, at last forgiven by Thomas, that I had a friend; that I had finally met someone whom I would never let down, looking to give, liking it for the giving.

"What can I do?" he said as I started squeezing the oranges.

Nothing. Nothing can be done. It was in the nature of the union that the one who turned his back on the other must be dropped. Nothing. It's over.

"Call her," I heard myself saying. "Talk to her, see her."

"I'll do what I can," he said, almost docile.

I gave him the number. He called. She hung up.

"Does she have a roommate?"

"A lovely one. You'll be crazy about her."

"I'm not interested in that and neither are you." He was annoyed at my bad faith.

Ten minutes later he called her roommate, an aspiring actress, and, yes, she would be only too happy to see him; it would be great.

If I had been disingenuous, I had not been lying: the roommate, Christine, was indeed lovely, a thin, soft, quiet blonde girl with a warm smile, strong bones, and clean, immense blue eyes. But she lived in a dark, cramped apartment, hardly large enough for one, and I doubted Mimi was happy there.

I said, "You wouldn't mind going to a hotel with me instead of staying here, would you, J.?"

I called Mimi, melting; first time with her voice in five days. Would she like to move back for a while? Jim and I would stay at the Hilton. Oh, yes, she would. Good.

In the taxi on the way downtown, the dimension of Brown's gesture, concern, began to come clear. He had sensed I was feeling bad, knew little more, and had traveled especially to New York to see if there were something he could do. Who was whose friend? What had I done, would I do, for him? We were stalled in the fetid, clamorous traffic of the afternoon, a fire crackling, disintegrating an office building nearby. Trapped between two trucks, the driver yawned and opened the *Daily News.*

"I really appreciate what you've done, J., I'm almost embarrassed; I don't really know what to say, how to thank you."

Uttered, the uneasiness was exorcised, transferred to him. He looked away.

"You'd have done the same for me." he said, quietly, firmly.

Would I?

I had known him, what? Two days? But he must have sensed a suggestion of future closeness, friendship, possibility; was making a major leap toward its realization now. Two days—no, not even that; he had sensed it that first moment when he looked at me and I looked away at the basket for a last, imaginary jump shot, when I hadn't yet known myself.

I would.

We took a suite at the Hilton, a plastic living room in red and yellow bridging two plastic bedrooms in white and brown.

"Look, I don't like leaving you alone, tying you down," said J., "but I think it's best if you stick around. If I can come up with something or if I learn anything that might help I'll call you right away."

"I'm not going anywhere."

It was eight o'clock. I waited for two hours, sitting on the couch, smoking, wrestling with my memory, pinning it to a recollection of my wedding: of my wife, fragile, sharp bones softened by gray eyes, a smile, a sigh— delicate, white lace flowing to the floor.

The phone rang. I leaped, was told angrily by a man's voice to put Janet on.

"She doesn't want to talk to you," I said.

"Let her tell me that," he said.

"Listen, I would, but she said she doesn't ever want to hear from you again."

"Put her on!" the voice shrieked.

"You had your chance but you blew it. It's too late now. If there hadn't been some fuck-up at the core of the feeling you wouldn't have ignored her when she was there. Talking to her now, or seeing her, or even getting her back wouldn't straighten that out; wouldn't straighten you out."

"Please," the voice said, "just let me listen to her." Then it cracked. It was choking, snorting, sobbing. Suddenly, I felt clear, miserable.

"Hey, wait! Actually, you have the wrong number. I don't know any Janet. This was only, you know, a joke. I was just playing along."

"A joke! What is this? Who are you? Where's Janet, you prick, where is she?"

I hung up, my head suddenly cramped with pain, a steel cylinder drilling my eye. I dialed the hotel operator.

"Excuse me," I said with exquisitely delicate calm, false to the marrow, "this is Mr. Toback. Did I happen to receive a call just now?"

"Pardon?"

"Did someone just speak to me on the phone?"

"Excuse me?"

"I mean, who was that?"

I hung up, called Mimi, waking her.

"Are you all right?" I said.

"Yes."

There was silence through the static of hazy connection. Then she clicked it. I lay still, waited another hour; then ordered dinner, ate a steak, cheese cake, salad; drank three Cokes. I turned on Johnny Carson: a fat, hideous woman introduced as a comedienne; a singer who finished "Ebb Tide" two bars behind the orchestra. I was debating the possibility of throwing one of the Coke bottles through the TV screen when the thought suddenly intruded upon me that Jim could walk on that show at any moment, uninvited, unexpected, and be welcomed gratefully by Carson, take the stage right away. I felt better; for J.B., O ego auxiliary, was working for me, Mr. C., massah, yes.

But where was he? It was one o'clock, and surely by now he must have heard, inferred, something. I paced the rooms, undressed, smoked, muttered, swore. I tried to sleep, but succumbed to the obsessions of insomnia: the accelerations, halts, horns of cars outside; the subdued monotony of radiator clicks; the aquatic commotions of the plumbing.

At three, I heard him come in. I scuttled across my bedroom, the living room, into his. He was sitting on his bed, pulling off his boots, apparently uninterested in talk. I checked my impulse to ask, stood. Finally, he looked up, eyes squinted in anger.

"Listen, I know how you feel, and it's not going to be easy for you to hear this, but I have to be straight with you." His voice was low, controlled; but short stops, breaths in the sentence, a broken, forced rhythm suggested irritation uneasily repressed.

"I don't think the question is whether you are or aren't

going to get Mimi back, I think it's whether you should or shouldn't."

"And you don't think I should," I said, accusatory, challenging.

"No, I don't know; and you don't really know, either. You need time. In six months—and I know that sounds like an impossible wait now—but if you feel in six months that you still can't stand being without her, and if she's missed you, too, then maybe you should. But right now, the only thing you can know for sure is that it's a lot of *other* factors that are bothering you—being left, instead of having done the leaving yourself; shame over having been dishonest; simple anger over not getting what you want; and maybe even frustration with the understanding that this is just the situation you were looking to bring on yourself—and Mimi—all along."

Sounds good, Siggy, I wanted to say, but sass and a smart ass would have got me nowhere; anyway, it was a heavy favorite he was right. I shifted the angle. "How did you like Christine?"

He shifted it back. "I upset her, I think. I just kept grilling her, trying to find out about Mimi, see what chances there were, and she didn't want to talk about it. Finally, she said that if that was all I'd come to see her for, she'd rather go home, and I realized she was right. And that I had been wrong. See (he looked down, shy), I think of you as a good friend, and when I saw you were low, it was a natural instinct to help. (Up again.) But what you think would help you and what would really help you might be completely different things. I went with your thing first, but then I dug, see, what really was obvious from the beginning: if there hadn't been some fuck-up in your feelings about her originally, you wouldn't have been looking to avoid her the way you did. (Watching me.) You wouldn't have come out to L.A. to meet me."

It all made sense. But, perhaps because I didn't want him to think he had wasted a trip, time, feelings, perhaps because I had never learned how to give up, in, without contention, even when wrong, perhaps from sheer perversity, I said, "Listen, a lot of what you said is true, J.; I know it. But I do dig her, I see it now; I know I'd still want her after she came back. I've learned, see."

"You've learned nothin' if you talk like that," he said, his voice hard. "This is an opportunity for you, Toe, you can build real control, find out a lot of shit about yourself, if you can be honest with it."

"Yeah." I waited.

He softened. "Look, I still want to help. But my way. Why don't you come out to L.A. and stay with me for a while? Don't call Mimi; tighten on yourself. Drop it here."

"I'd like to. I appreciate it."

We said good night, and I went to my room. If I had had a favorite literary concept, it was Keats's Negative Capability; it had always seemed the best, most exciting way to live, to revel especially in situations whose outcome was mysterious. I now would have another, more difficult, more interesting context in which to test it and myself. For the first time in a week, I slept well. In the morning I found a note saying, come when you're ready. I would; was.

Initiation

Brown was waiting for me when I arrived at the airport, parked outside in a new car, a chocolate-brown Mercedes 280 SL. He gestured lightly, and I climbed in. The door registered a clean, sonorous tone as I closed it, and it would have seemed natural to remark on it, or at least to make some general comment about the new car, but there was clearly something wrong, something else that needed to be said first, so I didn't. He looked straight ahead as he drove, played tapes of Marvin Gaye, stopped for gas and made a phone call. I sat stretched, my looseness assumed, smoking, waiting for him to make the move. It was not the ideal spirit in which to start a visit, and yet I felt an edge of curiosity, anticipation, which made me feel good to be there. When we turned off Sunset and started up the hill, no more than two miles now from his house, he spoke uneasily, rage restrained; eyes still trained on the road.

"I want to get one thing down so there's no mistake. You're here now, you're welcome and all; you can use the pool, the court, bring up friends, come and go as you like. It's your house. But you've got to carry your own weight. LeRoy Kelly's staying at the place now, too. He's got his thing, I've got mine, and you've got yours. When we're running together, that's cool; but when we're alone, we can't be thinking about who else needs what. You've got to take care of yourself."

"Absolutely. It goes without saying."

"Okay, then," he said, genuinely softer now, almost apologetic. "I just wanted it clear so everything would be straight from the start."

The night spent over Mimi had left its mark. But I was glad about it, and I understood now what had appealed to me in the silence, the cold thrust of the ride, understood beyond question my motives in having come back again. If, in my own eyes at least, perhaps even in others', I could be good here, hold my own with a man who was bigger, stronger, quicker, more sexual, *blacker* than any I would ever find, if I could make of this microcosmic world something richer, more complicated, sharper, then there would be no other in which I'd feel unable surely, proudly, to move if I wanted to. Acting on the assumption that, in America, Negroes, through suffering, endurance, the development and transmission of the strongest national style, and the deepest penetration into mythology and folklore, had finally become burdened with the priesthood that served the last, essential rites of initiation into manhood, I was sure that this was where I had to be. It was not inconceivable that the American Caucasian could never achieve maturity—as an individual or as a citizen of his country—until he had learned to exorcise his revulsion, his dread of darkness, until he had learned to fight, to live with, to love, to *become* black. So I welcomed, wanted, would, if necessary, *invent* the opportunities for participation in that rite.

I did not have long to wait. Hardly unpacked, settled in my room on the second floor, I was confronted by Jim in a black silk t-shirt, black shorts with a gold "32" stitched on the front, and sneakers. Was I ready for tennis? Well, yes, of course, I'd just change and be right with him. Tennis! Shit, I had just come off a plane. Still, I couldn't complain. Tennis had been my game for twenty years, the one sport in which I had shown real promise (however lamentably unfulfilled), and Jim had literally never held a racket in his hand until a month before. Moreover, he had avoided lessons, preferring simply to seek advice from old amateur sources on various specific points (such as how to grip a backhand, how to stroke a forehand) and then to inform them with his own instinctive athletic rhythm.

I came down in jeans and a yellow dress shirt, carrying my steel racket, and Jim, with a wood, immediately wanted to know what the advantage of steel was. Well, it was lighter, so you could whip it around more quickly, and its shape lent it good resistance to the wind and it glowed in the dark like a Tom Mix gun handle. He looked as unconvinced as I sounded.

"I have a theory about equipment in sports. Performance should always be a few steps ahead of it. It should always be kept at its simplest, minimum level until—and only if—a stage of fantastic achievement is reached. The more paraphernalia outdistances ability, the funnier and more pathetic a cat is. Your reasons seem like bullshit. I bet it doesn't make any difference at all."

"Probably not," I conceded. "But maybe I've reached a stage of fantastic achievement."

Jim laughed. "Maybe. Anyway, the weird thing is it doesn't jibe with your clothes. You don't have on neat whites with monograms and shit, and that's cool, because there's usually a whole clothes thing that goes along with the equipment obsessions. Cats who buy the most expensive baseball gloves usually look to cop spokes and a uniform. Shit, go with what you have; that's all you're gonna make it or blow it with anyway."

I agreed. It had, in fact, always been a matter of principle with me to avoid traditional tennis attire, even to flout the game's decorum, thus introducing the possibility of increased satisfaction if I won (my opponent's Fred Perry shorts or Lacoste shirt having initially suggested superior professionalism to him and to everyone watching), or diminished shame if I lost, since I was obviously the underdog, apparently intended by background and station to be routed. The display of wealth entails certain obligations of style and talent which, if unrealized, create an image of spoil and waste so sickening as to suggest that poverty would be a preferable condition.

In the car, cruising in search of public courts, Jim said: "I hope you know I'm not looking for competition yet. I just want to hit for the time being, and if you can help in certain areas, I'd appreciate it."

I could and would, but wished he hadn't said it; wanted there to be blades all over, every day, in everything; especially situations in which mine had been sharpened over an extra score of years. Still, this new role laid claim to its own interests and rewards. If only for a few hours, learner was to assume the role of teacher.

The place was empty when we arrived, four green asphalt courts, and we took our sides.

"Hold on a minute. You can't play now."

I turned and saw a short, frail, white-haired man limping toward us.

"Don't you see the puddles?"

"Sure," I said, "that's okay."

"It ain't okay. What's going to happen if you fall on that? You could break a leg and sue the city blind. We ain't protected."

"We'll be careful," I said. I was not about to lose my shot once it was so close at hand.

The old man shook his head.

"Not today."

I noted that Jim was silent throughout, characteristic reserve in responding to a new milieu. He would case a joint out before judging it or acting. Now he would accept any verdict, go if he had to. My disappointment must have registered, because the old man, after a long wait, decided that if we wiped the courts dry—he had the brushes—we could see how it worked. We went at it for ten minutes, a healthy sweat already covering my face and chest, and then began.

The anticipation, the sweeping labors, had pushed me to an early pitch of excitement and I began pounding the ball with a fervor somewhat excessive for any pregame rally, particularly for one in which the opponent's avowed goal was practice and instruction.

"Big Jim! Why are you hitting so hard? Don't be so aggressive."

All right. But I was anxious to get on with the match; anxious, because I had failed to see any indication in his strokes of the novitiate: his forehand was firm, reliable, and often deep; his backhand soft but accurately placed; his movement around the court distinguished by a grace and effortless quickness ordinarily the mark of professionals or, at worst, the most accomplished weekend amateurs. I wanted to see precisely where my edge lay, how I was going to qualify as leader and coach.

The first set failed to yield any answers. In the opening game, eager to establish superiority of strength, I tried to blow each serve by him. A single ace, however, was resoundingly negated by three double faults and I ended the game with a backhand crosscourt volley angled into the wire fence on the side of the court. It was not until three points later, however, that I came to understand that—his disclaimers notwithstanding—Brown was close to being an equal adversary on the court. Ahead 30-15 on his serve, and noting that the serve was still essentially a defensive tool for him, a means of setting up a rally rather than of establishing charge, I decided to attack it. The ball passed across the middle of the court on my forehand side, and I lashed it low and deep to his backhand corner, spinning it away from his movement. He stretched, snapped the racket back, and punched it deep down the line, a foot safe either way, past me as I arrived at the net to wait for what I had assumed—in the absurd possibility that he might manage to return the ball at all—would be the clinching blast.

"Beautiful! Fantastic shot! That's incredible, J. You're hitting winners already."

If I sounded happy, I wasn't. When he won the next two points by returning each of my efforts to pass him, I knew I was going to have no mental energy to expend on advice or correction for the benefit of his game.

Trailing 3-2, I began to be bothered by the sun, which was setting in my line of vision whenever I looked up to serve or to hit an overhead off his lobs. That we had not changed sides on odd games and that I had seemed to accept that each of us would remain where he was throughout the match would have made a sudden sugges-tion of shifting appear a sour excuse. Still, the conditions had taken hold of me, and, more, I was developing a large blister on the thumb of my right hand. At 4-5 and 30-40, game point for Brown on his serve, the thrust of what was happening abruptly took effect. Another mistake, and a whole set would be gone; 7-5, 6-0 would be pardonable—a new court, a long layoff, early stiffness; but 4-6 followed by anything, even two love sets in succession would estab-lish a parity that Brown had neither sought nor desired, and that I, as a result, was unwilling to concede. The ball came in close on my backhand, and I sliced it down the line in his forehand corner, followed to the net, and braced for a backhand volley placement. A lunge, a hard whip across his body—the first tap of any of his resources of power—and the ball crossed hard by me. I dived for it and missed.

"Wow!" I tried to sound excited. "Great shot! Fantastic set!"

"That's the set?" he asked, starting to smile. "It's over?"

"Right. Now we've got two more. Two out of three."

"You going to take me at love in this one?"

"Yeah. I have to."

Had to for whom? If I lost the next set I would need seriously to consider leaving L.A. that night. Not, I was coming to see, because of any burden of proof laid upon me by my host, but because I was simply unwilling to accept my stay, my relations with Jim, on terms of easy friendship. I had to be tested, to test myself for my own sake, and if I were to lose, if I were to fail at my own game, I would have to exact some price from myself in return.

Stakes established, I forgot about the glare, incipient blisters, and humiliating start, and pulled myself together for a run of four games. I served hard, followed fast to the net, volleyed sharply and deep and ran Jim into hitting from unnatural positions. In the fifth game, he took to lobbing whenever I came to the net, soft, deep lobs, tantalizingly low, but each somehow just beyond my leap and racket stretch. I would not be able to coast, would have to tighten on every point if I was to win.

The set ended 6-2 and I had regained a measure of my confidence. But in the third set I couldn't break away. I was trying to win with power, to dazzle as I had tried to dazzle in basketball, but he was acquiring the intelligence of the game as the match proceeded, learning what combinations of two—even three—returns were likely to draw me into errors, running me, playing a soft but unremittingly steady game; and I was committing mistakes at costly moments, and we arrived, as evening came, at a tie, 5-5. The old man appeared, said he would have to be on his way soon, so could we finish up, say, within five minutes? Time for two more games, and I would have to win both of them for even a minimal sense of my own belonging.

Jim served the first one, and I managed to stay a point ahead through seven points, arriving at advantage. The light was fading, the balls were dark with soot, and it was becoming increasingly difficult to see. I decided to gamble on a run of winners. The serve came in shallow to my backhand, and I whipped it crosscourt deep to Jim's backhand, trailing it. He placed it delicately down the line, and I lunged desperately, barely edging a forehand volley off the top of the net, then over. He swamped the middle of the court in one huge, powerful leap, scooped a lob over my head to the forehand side. I swung blindly and missed completely, then turned around and swiped again. I heard the steel edge of my racket collide with the ball, then saw it drop short, midcourt, at Jim's backhand. He pushed it deep into my forehand corner; I retreated and struck the ball cleanly, viciously, crosscourt. I loosened, sure of a winner, but then, incredulous, watched him stick out his racket and block it at a line straight at me. I shifted around it in panic, whipped again, once more hitting cleanly, this time right to his forehand, and he punched a volley to the baseline on my backhand. I drew back, murderous now, threw all the steel of my thigh up through my ass, into my chest, my arm, shooting the ball across the net, wide to his left, six inches inside the line.

"Beautiful, Toe! Just beautiful!" I doubt that he would have been more excited if he had hit the shot—won the point and game—himself.

"Thanks." I was drained.

I pulled ahead 30-love in the next game, the last no matter whose, but then served long four times in succession, to put him even. Was I expecting to lose? Looking to? If the fantasy was there, could the reality be far behind? Scared, I hit, consecutively, two of the hardest serves I have ever hit, both good, each an ace. I had won the game. The set was over and the match.

In the car on the way back I said: "I'd be on my way to Siberia if I had lost."

Jim laughed.

"I mean it."

"Are you serious?" He was unbelieving, appalled.

"Yeah."

"Wow!"

"Wow what?"

"Why is that? I just wanted a workout. I just wanted to make you fight. I wasn't out to beat you."

"That's the point. If you *had* been, I could have accepted it. But this is my game in relation to you—for now, anyway—and if I had lost, the only reason possible would have been that I wanted to. Still may be true, but by winning I at least put up an argument against it."

"I see what you mean," said J. Brown, not entirely convinced. "I dig."

Alfie's and The Candy Store

The next afternoon, I went with Jim for lunch to Alfie's, a hamburger café on the Strip, frequented by actors, athletes, agents, girls between jobs, hustlers of every variety. Most of the people were dressed casually, in bright colors—balloon-sleeve shirts, flared pants, beads, brassy belts, buckled shoes, boots. But next to us, at a corner table, there were three men, about forty, in plain t-shirts and worn jeans, or khakis, untouched by the air of forced good cheer, ivory smiles, incessant laughter that pervaded the rest of the place. The obvious leader, bigger, stronger, more sullen than his companions, looked like a truck driver or construction worker: thick arms, sturdy neck, heavy chest, broad shoulders, a hard swollen stomach suggesting long years of alcohol. His hair was combed forward to cover a deep recession in the front; his face was lined, a clean, crescent scar under his chin. His nose was fleshy and crooked, his lips tight; but the most remarkable part was his eyes—large, empty brown eyes, unfocused, angry; connotative of unrecovered shell shock. He stared at Brown's back as his friends and I studied him.

"Hey," he grunted suddenly, "you're Jim Brown, aren't you?"

Jim turned around and said, that's right, he was.

"Well," he said, standing up, "I'm Hawk Raymond and I want to shake your hand 'cause you been a hero of mine for a long time."

He reached out; Jim, sitting, took it.

"Hey," he said, moving closer, "you've got some fuckin' grip, you know that?"

Jim didn't answer.

"You know, I'm a fighter. I mean I used to be, but..." He shrugged, finally letting go, then pulled his chair over, up against Jim's, and sat down.

"Listen," he said in Jim's ear, almost whispering. "You know Big Train Lincoln? Well, I had him out on his feet in the first round in '59. We were just amateurs then, but I had him beat. Then he slipped under a right when I had him pinned to the ropes and he hooked me in the head like this. (He pushed his large knuckles against Jim's right temple.) And I couldn't even, I didn't even know...I woke up in the fuckin' locker room."

He stared miserably at the table as if he had just that moment learned of his loss. Abruptly, he put his hand on Jim's arm, running it up and down, squeezing.

"You've got some fuckin' arms." Suddenly, with his left hand, he slapped down on Jim's neck, felt it all around.

"Looka that neck, for chrissakes. You got the neck of a fuckin' bull!"

Jim, immobile, said quickly, "Let's see: you've checked out my hand, my arms, my neck. Next thing, you'll be checking out my jaw."

Hawk drew in his stomach and tightened his arms: "You think I'm scared to? You think you're too tough for me? Well, I'll tell you something, you're not. I ain't scared a shit! You got that? So don't go thinking you can scare me, boy, 'cause you can't. I'm in *shape!*"

He waited.

"Hey, you don't believe me? You want to try me out?"

"Hell no, Hawk." Jim looked up at him for the first time. "I'm no fighter, and I sure don't want to mess with you. I can see you're still very strong."

Hawk loosened, at ease for the first time now. Then he smiled, winked, and went back to his table and his friends.

Later, walking out, Jim was stopped again, this time by two Negroes, one tall and thin to the point of malnutrition, dressed in a brown iridescent suit, the other not much more than five feet, wearing a beret. The tall one was holding a batch of *Muhammad Speaks* newspapers.

"Would you care to help the Cause, brother?"

"No, thanks," Jim said, walking by.

The tall man grabbed his arm.

"Listen, this is for all black people. Anything will help. Ten dollars, five, a dollar."

"Look," Jim said, breaking loose, "I've got my own organization and my own ideas on how to help. So whatever I give, I put into that."

He started away.

"You *are* Jim Brown, aren't you?" the beret asked.

"What difference does that make?" The voice was hard, angry. "I explained my situation to you, and it holds, no matter who the fuck I am." The tall Muslim backed off.

"Say hello to brother Elijah for me," Jim called to them, and smiled.

On the way to his car, he said: "I understand that cat Hawk; he's a jock. He probably spent years lifting weights, running laps, sparring, hurting, all to make his body strong so he could think of himself as a man. That's what manhood meant to that cat, and even if it's a pretty shallow view, it's all he had. Then he sees a cat like me, who represents all sorts of possibilities in his own life that he never reached and now knows he never will. So he feels he has to challenge me. And I'd have to be pretty cruel to put him down. You just don't do it.

"But those Muslim cats pissed me off. Did you dig that 'You *are* Jim Brown' shit? The only thing they could hope to get from their angle is for me to feel guilty and give in or embarrassed and give in. And nobody's gonna do *nothin*' good for *those* reasons."

He drew a tape from the glove compartment and snapped it into the stereo.

"I'm not in the habit of taking rock lyrics seriously, but I want you to dig the words to this song, 'cause they say something very important better than anything else I know."

People say I'm the life of the party
'Cause I tell a joke or two;
Although I might be laughing loud and hearty,
Deep inside I'm blue.

So take a good look at my face,
You'll see my smile looks out of place;
If you look closer it's easy to trace
The Tracks of My Tears.

If you see me with another girl
Actin' like I'm havin' fun;
Although she may be cute—she's just a substitute,
You're the permanent one.

So take a good look at my face,
You'll see my smile looks out of place;
If you look closer it's easy to trace
The Tracks of My Tears.

Outside I'm masquerading,
Inside my hope is fading.
I'm just a clown
Since you put me down,
My smile is my make-up
I wear since my break-up with you.

Baby, baby take a good look at my face,
You'll see my smile looks out of place;
If you look closer it's easy to trace
The Tracks of My Tears.

I wondered—the memory of Mimi still clear in my mind, the evening at the Hilton still in Jim's—how coincidental the choice could have been. Thought of connecting the words of my situation, but didn't. Decided, instead, at that moment to put it finally out of conversation. An official, symbolic farewell.

"A cat could be singing that, too," I said.

"There've been times I could be singing that," said Jim.

The restraint had been repaid, a tacit deal transacted, community implied. I felt good driving home.

The Candy Store is (or was, as late as 1969)—the most desirable discothèque in Hollywood, which is to say that it was private—members consisting of movie stars, television personalities, show-business entrepreneurs, rock singers, and agents: those who had carved their initials on the buttocks of pop America—and that it had, every night, pretty California girls. Had, indeed, become the most notable manifestation of an institution catering to the western cult of Youth. One could come to exhibit oneself, to dance, to look (at or for), to drink, to hustle, to sit in fantasy or dream. One could wager with confidence that on any given night in any given city the majority of people ruled by vanity, petty ambition, sexual obsession, and social fashion would be crowding discothèques.

And yet there was more than a little to be said for them. It is difficult to think of any public meeting place in America where races and sexes mix more comfortably, where repressions and fears learned over a period of long years are so suddenly, naturally, forgotten. And provided one is in the right place on the right night, it is equally difficult to imagine a more pleasant setting in which to meet someone. Jim, informing me that he goes to a discothèque nearly every night, no matter what city he's in, takes me there, wearing a black dashiki with yellow and red embroidery, tight, sharply flared blue pants and black boots, and a heavy gold medallion with a naked woman on the face of it, hanging from his neck.

"It's a funny thing with this medallion," he says, smiling shyly. "Everyone thinks it's real gold, some exotic treasure I found in Calcutta or something. I bought it in a five-and-dime store."

He is greeted by the owner, waitresses, people at the bar. Warren Beatty, sitting with twins in identical dresses, jumps up to shake hands and say hello. We move past the dance floor to the back of the long narrow room, sit at a small table. Jim rarely drinks, orders rum and Coke; I don't at all, order Seven-Up. It's a quiet night for The Candy Store, he says. Not many girls alone. Not any, in fact, except two who are sitting together, across from us, to our left. We look at each other, smile, and go over to ask them to dance. They are both blonde and very young, sixteen probably, with short, turned-up noses and blue eyes, sweet, pretty faces. Enough alike to be sisters. I ask; they aren't. "Everyday People" is playing, and the four of us dance in a corner of the floor. Jim starts slowly, the suggestion only, of movement, watches for his girl's time, smiles, feeling it, seeing it there with his, launches into freer form, knees bending, shoulders dipping, fingers popping. I notice that half the people in the room are watching him, imagine it must always be so, wherever he dances. We go two more, then take the girls to our table.

"Why don't you come up to Jim's with us," I say. "It has the loveliest view of L.A. you've ever seen."

A line cut for high-school sophomores, which, it emerges, they are; they say, yes, they'd love to, but can't stay long because they have to get home, home to Orange County and their parents. *The baddest of bad spooks, O evil, unrepentant J.B., defiler of the sacrosanct and the pure, blackener of the white, soiler of the clean, trespasser on the purest of properties, hurler off balconies, Joe Frazier of the boudoir, O Negro de Sade! What pain will you wreak, what agony on this delicate Orange, pale and unripe?*

"What are you studying in school?" Jim asks, driving back. "Do you do much homework? Do you like it? I'm glad she's with us, Toback. She seems like the nicest girl I've met in a long time. Isn't she fantastic?"

She is. Her voice is soft and she listens to every word. Her friend listens to her listening.

At Jim's house we do look at the view from the pool: the lights, thousands of them, glittering, crackling below. You were right, she says, it is the loveliest view she has ever seen.

Jim puts on the Temptations; I sit with the other girl. Jim dances with the sweet one, teaches her some steps, new moves.

"Damn! You catch on fast," he says, and is truly excited and happy. "She's got such a good time. Hey, big Jim, you ever seen a girl so young keep such good time?"

No, I haven't; hadn't; still haven't.

"The great thing about black people," she says to Jim when the record is over, "Is that they've got—you've got—got such, um, *rhythm.*"

No snigger, not even a chuckle from Ebony J.; just a smile, a touch of her cheek.

But my gosh! We're so late. Oh, gee whiz! We have to go. And they do after calling a taxi and several fond good-byes.

"You know," he says, "I used to feel every girl I went out with had to be a virgin."

The ultimate possession, the possession of the past, of moments you never knew about or shared.

"And even though I've grown away from that, there's something so soft and good about this girl; maybe only a virgin can have it. And, damn, what a dancer! What time! A chick is seventy-five percent there already if she can dance like that."

I mention Sir John Davies and the Renaissance idea of dance as the most revealing expression of personality, the surest means of cultivation and refinement, the act through which the polarities of the human temperament—aggression and tenderness, arrogance and modesty, baldness and subtlety, abandon and control—are uniquely reconciled; an idea with which I'm coming to agree. Quote him the central stanza from *Orchestra*.

> Dancing, bright lady, then began to be
> > when the first seed whereof the world did spring,
> The fire, air, earth, and water did agree
> > By love's persuasion, nature's mighty king,
> To leave their first discorded combating,
> > And in dance such measure to observe,
> As all the world their motion shall preserve.

He is interested, impressed; says he's had the same feelings about it himself but hadn't know of Davies and would like to learn more. I am happy over this notion, over the suggestion of a new, fluid role; the thought that I, too, will be able to teach and to give.

The Black Economic Union

The Day of the Locust. The Burning of Los Angeles. Poverty. Sweat. Hunger. Funk. Junk. Murder. Heat. Pawnbrokers. Flames. Fire.

My vision of Watts had been a pastiche of television and newspaper accounts, political speeches, an occasional novel, propaganda black and white. But now, driving through it with Kenny Morris, Jim's troubleshooter for the BEU, it looked immeasurably prettier, more relaxed, than Harlem, Chicago's South Side, any other black inner city I had ever seen. Reasonably spacious and green, the buildings with room to pose, the sounds—soul from a record store, cars speeding and stopping, conversations in the street—nicely autonomous, resisting impingement upon each other.

Morris is a short, light Negro, about thirty, with processed hair and thick glasses; dressed for comfort rather than style, drives a battered '66 Mustang; has quick smart eyes, a wide, frequent smile. His voice is soft and he speaks clearly, balanced reasoned sentences constructed on neat syntax, acquired rhythms.

"Jim's image is founded mainly on sex. His life is supposed to be an orgy from one end of the earth to the other. And I'm not saying that he isn't a sexual cat. But what people don't realize is that, aside from football and movies, he's one of the great businessmen in this country. In two years he has developed a film company, a clothing chain, a hair-products company, a nightclub, a record company, a coffee company, and a management agency for rock groups.

"Take the coffee. In New York, Twenty One draws the most successful white people in the city for lunch and dinner, right? And they must drink a few hundred pots of coffee a day at a dollar a pot, right? Well, every pot is Jim's.

He got together with a cat in New York called Buddy Gist, and they developed and marketed an arabica blend from Tanzania which they called 'Kilimanjaro,' and already, in a year, they supply Twenty One and sell in delicacy shops all over the country. And Jim don't even drink coffee.

"Or take the record company. The Friends of Distinction is one of the biggest groups in the country now, and Jim has been with them from the beginning. He got them together, exposed them, booked them all over, and arranged their contracts.

"Or Maverick's Flat. It draws the hippest people in Watts every night. Jim drops in from time to time, but essentially it represents another investment.

"Most businessmen would be happy to have any one of these deals going for them. The coffee guy would define himself as the owner of a coffee company, the rock manager as a recording executive, and the nightclub owner would be in his place every night. But these are just side games with Jim, no matter how successful. And he doesn't even trade on his name. It's no short-term fling which would die overnight if his fame suddenly cooled."

It was impressive: Brown had played at white games in his spare time and beaten the sweatiest of his single-minded competitors with casual anonymity. Still, I wasn't satisfied. As Morris talked, I felt the same uneasiness I had sensed listening to Jim talk about the BEU. I didn't know exactly what disappointed me about it, what even *annoyed* me in this celebration of black capital and economic regeneration, this business orientation and product-consumer conversation, but I knew that it was not what I wanted to hear.

"But the beautiful thing is that Jim sees—and has taught all of us to see—that, especially for a black man, personal success (in sports, movies, or business) is hollow unless it's applied on a national scale to help all black people, all the brothers and sisters. Hey! You can hear it in the language, man. Black cats who are really hip to what's happening will always speak of brothers and sisters, because, collectively, historically, they and their ancestors have endured so much pain and persecution and humiliation and joy together that it feels as if they—as if *we*—were all part of the same family.

"The BEU may not be as exciting as the Panthers or as tough as the Rangers or as well known as SNCC or as rich as the NAACP. But it has given a shape to the life of everyone who's part of it and to hundreds of other groups and people who've looked to it for help. It's a cliché, but, fuck it, we've found our identity through Jim.

"Take me, man; I got a BS at UCLA in criminology, but I decided against the FBI for the same reason that any black man who doesn't want a skin transplant would decide against it. Instead, I went to work in the production department of Paramount. It paid well, but from my office window I used to watch white company executives playing tennis every afternoon at a club across the street where I would have been welcome mainly as a janitor. So I came to see that only certain doors in a white company will open for a black man, no matter how glad it is to hire him. Even if I weren't counting on someday running Paramount—or the FBI—I would have liked to know that I could have if I had deserved to. And as it stands in most white organizations today, I couldn't, no matter what. So I was ready for a change, and when Jim came up with his offer, I went with the BEU as a fieldworker. The salary isn't up to what Paramount paid, but at least I feel useful." He stopped, smiled. "Sometimes even indispensable."

"Spencer Jourdain, the cat who's in charge of the New York office, has a similar story. He graduated from Harvard and walked right into a beautiful job at Corning Glass. But he felt as out of place there as I did at Paramount. It was a dead end. So he took less than half the bread and went to work for Jim.

"Or the Flea—Walt Roberts. That's the cat you'll be meeting at the office."

"I know all about him," I broke in. I felt better; at last I would be talking some football to a hip freak, to a spook who was what a spook was cut out to be: quick, good-looking, mean, hard. I had watched him for several years with the Browns, their fastest runner, sharp feline moves, an exceptional wide receiver.

"When Cleveland traded him to New Orleans, he had his best year ever. He led the team in scoring and pass catching, and the Saints weren't good enough even to dream of letting him go. But they did, and the reason they did was that he had taken on Jim and the UAA to represent him. NFL owners have a different idea of Produce, Achieve, and Prosper from Jim's. They don't throw parties over the notion that a black cat is on the organizational, managerial end of contract negotiations. So there was the Flea, at twenty-six, with at least six good lucrative years ahead of him, out of a job with nowhere to go, and it looked pretty bleak.* But he'd learned from the experience that even in a game which depends for its existence on black participation, a black cat can get fucked for turning to another black cat. So he went to Jim again

* Walt Roberts played the 1970-1971 season with the Washington Redskins, only because of the undauntable integrity of the late Washington coach Vince Lombardi.

and adjusted from the role of a well-paid football star to a hundred-dollar-a-week functionary. It wasn't an easy transition, but Walt's smart and he has worked his balls off. Now he's the head of the L.A. office."

We pulled up on South Vermont Street. The office was the inconspicuous ground floor of a small gray building, flanked by dry cleaners, soul-food stands, record shops, clothing stores. I followed Morris into a small room with several desks, a few chairs, photographs of Brown, plaques, cabinets, papers, typewriters. On the wall was the motto: Produce, Achieve, Prosper. *Eat, Drink, Be Merry. Touch, Kiss, Love. Hit, Run, Score. Ribs, Chicken, Watermelon.*

A secretary walked in from a back room and greeted Morris, who introduced me. A moment later, Roberts entered. He was unbelievably small for a football player, looked to weigh no more than 160, lean, tapered. We shook hands.

"Jim's doing an article on Jim," Morris said, "and he wants to take a quick taste of the office."

"Well, I guess it's not much to look at," said Roberts. His voice was soft, nearly to the point of inaudibility. "But it's the work that counts, and there's plenty of that. I've just been packaging these medallions we're going to be selling."

He removed one from around his neck. It was dull gold, a large round face with the figures of Tommy Smith and John Carlos carved in their fist-brandishing power-salute pose.

"The idea is that their number at the Olympics had meaning way beyond its immediate effect. It was the first time black athletes, who are supposed to be grateful patriots, had taken a strong unified stand of protest. It was a symbolic thing that young black people will be able to look back to with pride, and emulate for years. It took great courage, too, because both of them knew that by going through with it they would have a hell of a time getting anywhere in professional sports, let alone in the business or endorsement line that's usually open to star athletes.

"We thought that a medallion commemorating the act would have a lot more relevance to black cats than, say, a St. Christopher's medal or love beads. Also, manufacturing these things sets an example of the kind of independent production black people can develop on their own; and it won't hurt the BEU treasury any, either. We're selling them for four dollars each."

"Whose idea was it?" I asked, forcing interest.

"Mine. But Jim's the one really responsible for all of it, either directly or indirectly. The organization means everything to him. It's his whole life. It has saved him, Kenny, me; thousands of others. And he's going to keep it growing, helping more; he's going to make it work."

There was a hard glow in Roberts' face as he spoke, eyes widening, flashing. And suddenly, I couldn't hear him anymore, my mind was off, days behind, thirty miles away, back in Brown's kitchen, and I was hearing him again, talking about Green Power and the Muslims, the UAA and Karenga; I was seeing him again, hands plowing his hair, heavy, solid frame close to supine on his chair. And I was hearing the reverberation of my own thoughts: *far away from himself, white...the Ford Foundation...He wishes he were with pussy now, always, that's all; he's just...outta caps, you outta caps.*

But who, really, wanted the pussy? Whose mind, bored, was wandering? Who was out of caps? Who, at bottom, were the white reporters, businessmen, *Esquire* editors, housewives, football players and owners, sheriffs, who saw a big, bad, evil spook, joint cocked, ready to ravish their ladies and rule America? And who, a few minutes before, had been able to absorb only the surface of Kenny Morris' eloquent words? Roberts was still talking, but I only saw his lips moving, didn't hear a sound. For who, after all, had been stunned to find Jim Brown six feet two and 225, thinking, psyching his opponent Toback off the court? And who had come three thousand miles to penetrate a world, a world, finally, imagined, nothing but his own, carried that distance in his head, projected on another, preconceived?

"You're soaked," Roberts said. "Do you want a towel?"

"No, I'm okay."

There was a long pause. I was hoping the phone would ring.

"Listen," I said, rushing. "I'd really like to join if I can. What do I have to do?"

"Well, a small donation would help, anything you can spare."

I wrote a check for an amount considerably beyond what I could afford and gave it to him.

"Hey! This is wonderful."

"I want some medallions, too. I'll buy about twenty and try to sell them when I'm back in New York."

I thanked, excused, left. Outside, on the way back to Jim's, the box was bulky and uncomfortable under my arm.

Notes on Partying

The order and form of the next week is blurred in my memory. I can see and feel incidents in vivid detail, but sequence and context are indistinct.

1. It is a warm night, stars rich and large, smoke rising outside from the heat of the pool. Jim is in his bedroom, door locked; no word about what he's doing or planning. Kelly is sitting on the living room sofa, playing solitary blackjack. I join. I like the feel of that, blackjack with the best back. Black black Buck back Boot black with Toback. We play for pennies, then dimes, quarters, dollars; I lose. Kelly's got good bones, an angular, oval face, the sclera luminous buoys in a spook-dark sea of skin. No lines, no tension, no suffering there, and I feel easy in his company.

I rise to play some old tunes from the time when one danced slow, both hands tight on the girl's ass, two marvelous mountains of flesh, soft or firm, loose or tight, large or small, what difference did it make then as long as she permitted you—wanted you—to do it, her arms draped gently over your shoulders, fingertips tracing paths of chills on your neck, a nice pressure at the groin letting you know (O fabulous dream come true!) that soon you would be lying with her, naked, free to look at everything, to feel it next to you, to touch it, to move inside it, to bury yourself in it, reveling in it until you died; and that she (most wondrous of wonders!) wanted it, too, and just as much as you. What was she *doing*, that crazy girl, what letting herself in for, so brave and so bold, so transcendently beyond what you yourself could ever come to do? The excitement, the terror, the newness, the dirtiness, the cleanliness, the marvel, the beauty of it all!

I stack them: the Mello-Kings, "Tonite Tonite"; the Chantels, "Maybe"; Lee Andrews, "Teardrops"; Johnnie and Jo, "We Belong Together"; Don and Juan, "What's Your Name." Those three fast years of freshness and sheer delight, the joy of discovery, after the trunk had thickened and the apples fell. Flashing, I sit with LeRoy. LeRoy. *Hey LeRoy, Your Mamma's Callin' You.* Hey LeRoy. Hey boy. He LeRoy, she's callin' you, LeRoy, your Mama. Jimmy Castor. Yes, Jimmy Castor, that was the first time. Go back not thirteen years but nine and find that second seed, when innocence, or at least the illusory claim one had laid to it, was finally lost, when the ass had now to be tight and hard, the legs long and thin, the face soft and lovely, when *yes* was no longer celebrated but assumed, when anticipation had been spoiled by too much realization, when ecstasy had dulled to pleasure, and when pleasure yielded emphasis to exhibition. Jimmy Castor. I had brought a girl uptown to *Small's* one night—ten of us, all white. And Jimmy Castor, sax in his mouth, drumsticks in his fingers, voice in his throat, coils in his legs, had got to the girl, shot his rhythm thirty feet across the room and through her, down into her juices, catalyzing their flow. He would have her; she would have him. Not altogether remarkable, at first thought; but then, in the days following, everyone—I—wondered, dreamed, feared what had happened, what it was like, what *he* was like, tall, slender beanstalk of a spook, but spook, for the first time, a real live one.

She didn't need to say. Even if she hadn't gone back every night to hear him, moved in on him, needed him, loved him, the fantasy was in our minds.

"You're startin' the party early, I see," says LeRoy.

"What party?"

"Jim's. Ours. There's a party here tonight."

"No shit. Who? Who's coming? What girls, what

guys? Who?"

"Boom-Boom and J.D. are bringin' up the girls."

"Boom-Boom?"

"And J.D. They're an entry. You don't know them yet? Wow, Toback, you're in for a *thing*, boy. There ain't no one *any*where like Boom and J.D."

I feel as though I have just been hit with a nine on thirteen (the dealer showing ten), just watched the ball pop out of double-zero after laying my bottom dollar on it. I sense that I am approaching, now, finally, this night, the situations, recognitions, I have been waiting for, seeking all along, not only since meeting Jim (Brown) but since the time with Jim (Castor) and before. But I don't feel quite ready.

The bell rings. Timmy Brown, another former NFL running back, now a singer and actor, comes in, followed by Lenny Smith, Jon White. Timmy's short, lean, hard; skin light tan, oiled black rings of hair, a sweet smile, a wholesome, pretty face, nice warm shake of the hand. Lenny, an actor, entertainer, construction worker, is built like Jim, massive shoulders angling sharply down on a narrow waist, graceful, even gentle, of movement, as though far away, ever, from the possibility of calling upon the full resources of his strength. Jon is an actor, too, tall and very thin, wearing a denim suit, a black (I think to myself) Toback.

A handsome group, and one feels good moving in it. The mood is warm, relaxed, easy. I cannot remember ever having seen people—friends—more surely, uninhibitedly, unguardedly warm with one another. I feel the release of spirit extended to me; LeRoy introduces. I am admitted trustfully. But I still have my edge, a steel blade honed to cut, fantasies wild. *I see Kelly stomping a prostrate* tackler; Timmy butting a face, white, stepping on it with his cleats; Lenny pounding in a head, also white, several heads now, clouting with knuckles and heels; even Jon (who's almost aggressively quiet, with a mysterious, subtle smile cracking the edges of his mouth, slow, deliberate movements and gestures), even Jon blasting holes in bodies with a piece.

Jim comes in, dressed in long navy blue pants, a heavy flare, fitted to the muscles of his ass and thighs, a loose shirt open at the collar. Greetings, and then he sits down to chess with Timmy.

Bell again. This time the deluge. Ten, maybe twelve girls, a few very pretty, students, office workers, hippies, black and white, flood in; and at the rear a curious pair of men. A short, thick, starkly black man of about thirty, jeans cut away at the knee exposing immensely muscular calves, a round, beaming face, eyes gleaming with tricks and anticipation of fun; and with him a thin, lighter spook, long face bisected by a bushy walrus mustache, dressed head to toe in white, a yachting hat and shirt (with insignia), Levi's, sneakers, and socks. Salutations; introductions. The smaller one says to me, "I'm Boom-Boom, pleased to make your acquaintance, and this is my partner, J.D."

To which the taller one adds, "I'm J.D. of Hollywood, a yachtsman and jet setter, you see. I park my yacht in L.A. harbor, where the rich folk lay out. We jet setters hang together, see. Can you dig it?"

He laughs hysterically and then turns to one of the girls he has brought in, still, however, addressing me.

"This is Carol, who I just met and brought up to this lovely, quiet, elegant palace in the hills; and since you look like a fellow jet setter, New York (I'm going to call you 'New York,' O.K.?), I'd like to turn her onto you, because initiation, dig it, is the spice of life, a crucial phase of life in a new atmosphere, and I'd like to feel that you're having a ball right from the start in our lovely playboy's principality of Hollywood. Can you dig it, New York? Can you *dig* it? See, I appreciate fellow jet *setters*, New York; we Samoans and yachtsmen have to stick together and look out for each other and be mutual and friendly and loving and kind and present each other to the many lovely ladies of Hollywood that we meet from hour to hour in the due course of our allotted days."

J.D. whips out his palm and I slap it and I like him immensely, right out. Jim, his chess game temporarily interrupted, is laughing at J.D.'s act, an appreciative king to his court jester. J.D. speaks perpetually with a wide, almost maniacal smile, his voice forever testing the edge of a frantic giggle.

"You may wonder, New York, how J.D. and Boom-Boom of Hollywood always manage to cop the loveliest ladies in L.A. County. We look for their special quality, their elegance and grace of expression, the beauty of their mind, and the colors of their souls. Then we pay tribute to it, and to the shape of their legs, the richness and fleshiness of their titties, and the splendid splendor of their pussies. Then we hip them to what's happening: that this is Hollywood and that in Hollywood jet *setters* and yachtsmen love to eat pussy and run around naked and have wonderful pleasure with each other and make each other feel good. Can you *dig* it, New York, can you *dig* it?"

"I can dig it," I say, watching J.D.'s mustache and laughing.

"I like New York, Jim," J.D. says to Brown. "New York is a jet *setter*! Hey, Boom-Boom, dig it!"

The next recollection I have of that evening finds me

in my room with one of the girls Boom-Boom and J.D. have transported for celebration. She is a legal secretary with a quiet voice. Rhythms connected, bodies locked firm, exquisite tingles and shivers on my scalp, spine, fingers, and toes. But then I sense, behind me, on the terrace outside, something, a presence; I'm being watched. Head up, looking back: Boom-Boom and J.D. And suddenly I begin to apprehend, physically, what the whole visit means. The time quickens, hardens, into long, solid clouts, thuds. Tossing, throwing, pinning her legs. Whooping. Riding. (O.K., we've all heard something like that before.) But for how long? Past what limits of mere sensual gratification and desire? And for whom? I moan and want the girl—will bring her, going with her—to yell. I drive and want the girl—leading her—to thrash. For them, whipping me to extra strides, a long, brilliant, stretch, a crowbar up my ass; for them, because they have—buried somewhere in the recesses of America's myths, of mine, perhaps even of our truths—the real claims and keys to that simplest, sheerest primordial power, the source, of which all other forms of power are surrogates—pale, impersonal approximations.

A historical proposition: If a white slaveowner who held, say, twenty-five slaves, fifteen of them men, several with wives and daughters, could call at will upon any of their women—as his dehumanized possessions—to serve his sexual whims, could expropriate them regardless of their own or their husbands' or fathers' resistance and pain and humiliation, then what unremittable rage, transposed first subliminally, now literally, through generations, must have been harbored, checked, held uneasily at bay, in anticipation of the day when the *master's* woman, the inviolate lily, would be plucked, stolen, won, through superior efforts in the one game where the odds were even? And what fear, transposed historically, what awful guilt must have been passed among Caucasians? What suspicions, what knowledge, what fantastic exaggerations of that very urge in blacks? And what consequent projections, plans for protection and reaction to conserve their own women, to guard and to maintain the last vestige of their purity?

What, moreover, is the historical and psychological significance of the triangular relation of pimp, hooker, and john in contemporary America if not the realization of black revenge? The white prostitute, fucked, and so won, possessed, by the black man, will allure, nail, white men, lie passively or feign theatrically for them, then take their money and pass it on to her new "father," her "big daddy," the one who has *earned* her, her "old man." For the pimp, his posture has generated a racial reversal full cycle. If his grandfather had to wait, watch, while the master took his grandfather's wife, then he himself will live—eat, drink, dress, dance, drive—from the money the master's grandson pays him to have, and only fleetingly, the grandson's own symbolic wife.

Indeed, the bitterness felt by many whites over the partial effectuation of sexual retribution—as well as their continuing fear of its increase—has forced them into humor (or attempts at it), the last defense of the defenseless. The President himself, reflecting the taste of a major share of his (record-buying) constituents, requested a performance at the White House of Guy Drake's "Welfare Cadillac," a Country and Western hit song that mockingly asserts that "things are still gonna get better" because of "a whole new poverty plan," which will provide welfare recipients with enough money to buy Cadillacs. Drake further states, "If they ain't on welfare and don't drive a Cadillac, then I ain't talking about them." That the welfare money traditionally received by prostitutes is often passed to their pimps, and that black pimps are, as a group, the only Americans both using welfare funds and sporting Eldorados particularizes Drake's, Nixon's, slur; their slur, their squeamishness, their discomfort, their self-righteousness, their bathos, and their fear.

But for whom, I was asking, for *whom*? For whom the exhaustion of all my resources and rhythms, the need for control unparalleled, demonstrated beyond dispute? Not for her or for Boom-Boom or for J.D. or even, on the primary level, for me, but for J.B.; for it is his image, darkest of dark symbols, stunning, enlarged, his biggest and grandest presence, that I feel preying on my mind. As Boom-Boom and J.D. draw in, I pull out, downstairs, to see what's up, what *he* is up to.

Still playing chess with Timmy. The sounds around say none can take J.B. Here again. No one. Friends, amateurs, aficionados, competitors of all kinds have come up to beat him on the board and haven't. Timmy, quietly, shakes his head, is losing, will lose, has lost. I nod at J.B., hear a "Big Toe! What's happening?" Say: it's all fine. But I'm waiting for more, for his move, for him to lead an entry to his room, and to go myself, too. What I had felt, learned upstairs, whetted—didn't sate the appetite; punctured—didn't penetrate—the areas of feeling I needed to explore. It won't, however, happen now. He does lead an entry out, but alone, through the living room and hall, friends around him dancing, looking. I watch him go in, close the door.

An eye now to LeRoy, Lenny, Timmy: handsome, athletic spooks all. I notice a deference, a mood of acceptance, a willingness to take the lead from J. They are quick and smart, they've worked well, made a mark in their own games, would ordinarily run next to, or in front. But there's an attitude they share in relation to Jim, an instinct to listen before they speak, to anticipate when they answer, to seek, to blend, to understand, to follow. They are slightly on edge, slightly—always—in awe; not so much of his size or strength or talent or wit, of his achievement, the success and power he has developed, not even of his elemental blackness; but rather, of that extraordinary, intangible, unteachable quality that Nietzsche speaks of, the *genius of the heart*, that quality that I had felt from him, too, from the beginning, and that made me, at that moment, want to go through that door. I would need to wait.

2. Another night, another party; larger, louder, longer. The sense of ease, accessibility, is wonderful. People swim, dance, eat, make love, drink—naturally, joyfully. There is one incongruity: a young black singer, graceful, tall, emaciated, nonathletic, weak, gay to the border of hermaphroditism. One easily imagines him in drag— lipstick, wig, mini, and boots. Again, I watch Jim go off, accompanied by two, into his room, in his metered half limp; and again I wonder, wait. As dawn comes, the living room still crowded, I wander up to bed.

Close to sleep, locked in, there is a rap on my door. Soft, irregular at first; then deep, more penetrating, violent. "Jim, Jimmy, let me in! Let me in, boy, you hear, let me in! Open up. What are you doing in there?" It's he; I had spoken casually to him; about his records, his career, his clothes, my work. But now I am taken by surprise, scared.

"I'm falling out, man," I make the mistake of saying.

"I've got to get some sleep. I'm exhausted."

"Just let me come in for a minute."

His voice is held, hysteria and shrill cracks of laughter uncomfortably muzzled. "I just want to say good night to you, Jimmy, just a quick good night. Open the door! Please!"

The knock is harder.

"Good night."

"Oh come on, don't be a bitch. Just let me in for a little minute."

I shiver at the thought of the gay boy, of white ideas and ideals of black. This one is pathetic, a casualty of war, the debris from a tragic historical wreckage. And I understand now, more than before, Jim's insistence on manhood and on the upper hand, not the small-minded, mean-spirited call to "do one's thing," do it and fuck the world, but rather a desperately controlled sense of integrity, absolute fidelity at all times to the self that one has created, by which he has lived. For, with emasculation often a literal condition for blacks only two generations ago and a figurative one in the official culture even today, the slightest relaxation of principle, the mere suggestion of abandoning one's own strong impulse and personal code, endangers seriously the self that has been fortified only with the greatest of determination and care.

"Go away," I say firmly. Then I yell: "Get out!"

3. Boom-Boom and I meet two girls from UCLA at Chicken Delight. It is warm, early evening, and we take them to Jim's, swim in the pool, dance, eat, make love. After they leave, Boom-Boom says:

"Toback, you're a handsome boy, you get your words out right, you make your way with the ladies of Hollywood. But as you perhaps noticed, it was Boom-Boom's force that set it so everyone knew just what was going to happen. Now, how do you explain that? Boom-Boom is short, he's a little too stocky, he hasn't had a great deal of education, and you could fit all the money he has in this world into the wrapper of a candy bar and still have room for the candy. So how does he do it, not just tonight: all the time. What makes the ladies love Boom-Boom, want his mouth on their pussy, their mouth on his dick, his dick in their cunt? Are you ready? It's because of his big, fleshy, black lips, his deep, dark skin, and the fat length of big thing. A lady sees Boom-Boom and she sees *black*; she sees the lips, the skin, and the dick; and that's all. And I mean *any* lady—Princess Kelly, the grace of the Riviera, Jackie Kennedy of America and Greece, or Cleopatra of Egypt. That's all they see; that's all they want to see."

It's a brand of Eriksonian Negative Identity, kindred to Sartre's inauthentic Jew who locates his self-definition in terms conceived by the anti-Semite. I am interested to know how Brown would react to such a formulation, and I don't have long to wait. He arrives as Boom-Boom and I are shooting baskets under the lights in the driveway, and we follow him into the kitchen for some quarts of orange juice. I mention Boom-Boom's theory. Jim laughs his laugh, long. Then, "It's not entirely untrue for *some* white chicks, Boom. But it sure ain't right for others. Some go beyond it; some never get into it at all."

"I'll tell you about love," Boom-Boom says. "A sharp dude never bows to it. He retains his independence."

"Is Boom-Boom such a dude?" I say.

"He sure is. The lady doesn't *exist* who's captured Boom-Boom's heart. Too much pain there, Toback and J.B., too much trouble. I take my ladies, and then I send them off when the time comes; but they never possess me. Boom-Boom's too smart for that shit. Boom-Boom's too free. No lady *ever* hurt Boom-Boom, never broke his heart or led him by the nose."

Jim is approaching something like catatonic laughter.

"What are you laughing at, J.B.?" says Boom-Boom in mock anger and half horror.

"You've *never* been in love?"

"No."

"Never been led or possessed?"

"Never."

"And never hurt?"

"Not by a lady. Never have been and never will."

"Shake a hand, lawdy lawdy! Boom, you're somethin' else. Emerging unscathed. Boom-*Boom*."

"*Say* it," says Boom-Boom gleefully.

"I'll tell you what I'll say," says J.B. "If what you say is true (his eyes dancing, playing games with Boom) you're missin' a whole lot of good stuff."

"Jim Brown! You tellin' me you been hurt by a lady? You tellin' me that's a good thing?"

Laughs again; says: "I sure have. I sure am."

4. "Get dressed up, Toe. I want to take you to a party."

It's the first time I've gone *out* somewhere with Jim. Hollywood—the people he's interested in seeing—comes to him. He likes the comfort of the home court advantage.

We drive for a half hour, stopping to ask occasional directions, arriving at last in Benedict Canyon, I think, then up, past guards, to a pretty, red French farmhouse. Roman Polanski, the host, greets us, leads us into a rectangular situation, a hallway dividing to the left a long living room with a balcony running end to end above, and to the right a tidy buffet dining area, rich cream, straw-berries, wild colorful fruits decorating a brown table. Incense, candles, weed in the air.

There is a studied elegance about the people—forty, maybe—who move quietly, voices soft, across, in and out. Gypsy costumes on many of the girls, flower-pattern shirts on the men; everyone seems thin, graceful; draped over the edges of sofas, leaning against walls in corners, huddled, whispering on the balcony. The music is the Beatles, then a Brandenburg, both suiting the ambience. If Dionysus would prefer a party at Jim's, de Sade would feel more at home here. It has a white face, the only spooks besides Jim being Jimmy Baldwin and Richard Ward, a Negro actor I know from New York and with whom I speak now. Ward has a marvelous laugh, triggered accommodatingly by the mere approximation of humor. We get to reminiscing, and the laugh comes, bellowing, in waves, flooding the room, and, flat out, we have jumped the muted mood. A small, pale man of about twenty-five, listening with intense concern to tales of spiritual discovery told by an aging producer, glares up at us.

Jim is making his rounds, talking to different girls, avoiding, as he always seems to, stars. Jane Fonda is there and Sharon Tate, with warm greetings for everyone (unique here); but, again, that would be the obvious move, so Jim will make it his last.

I drift into an old friend, a delicate blonde girl of angled, Nordic beauty and consummate marketplace duplicity, and embark with her on an orgy, slightly strained, of mutual delight and surprise. Jim joins.

"You knew her before, Toe?"

"A long time."

"She's pretty. (She smiles.) But she's got cunning in

her eyes. Don't think she could be trusted too far. (She smiles more, laughs.) Right?" He laughs.

Jim has the habit of talking *to* you *about* a third person in front of that person. A tactic of self-protective indirection that is, also, more than a tactic, a form of honesty; for it is precisely what he would be telling you about her (or him) or telling her about herself if there were only two.

"Still, I like her; I'd love to see her up at the house."

"Why don't you come with us now?" I say.

At which point the pale, intense fellow springs up from behind and grabs her arm.

"This is my boyfriend, Bob," she says, blushing at his excitement.

I begin to remember.

"Maxwell?"

He grunts in affirmation.

"From Atlantic Beach?"

A brief nod.

"No shit! I'm Jim Toback."

I am all excited. It was Bob Maxwell who had served up the pitch that I hit for my fifteenth, record-breaking home run of the summer, fifteen years before in a Long Island hardball league. More, we'd often met at parties, spent time with friends at the beach, swum together, eaten hot dogs, drunk Cokes, hitched rides.

"Don't you remember? Jim Toback. We played baseball. Barbara Miller, Ricky Rose, Vicki Warwick, Philip K—"

"Yeah," he cuts in, mumbling. "I remember. That's a long time ago. I don't see any of those people anymore."

"I'm overwhelmed by your affection," I say.

"Let's get away from here," he says to the girl, and drags her across the room, she turning back to give a face shrug and to mouth a "Call."

"Wow!" says J.B. "Didn't like that. The sucker's *tight.* I don't want any trouble, Toe; no need for that."

I go back to Ward; Jim circulates some more, briefly, stops to talk to Polanski, then returns.

"Ready? Let's go play some tennis. I found out about some courts near the house where they have lights."

I'm not unhappy about it. I would prefer Boom-Boom and J.B., the girls from the Strip, good feelings, warmth, laughs, release, a freer field.

As we head out, Jay Sebring stops Jim. Says Roman wants him to stay.

"I know, but we've got a thing to take care of. It's been nice, though."

On the way back: "What was that about?"

"Polanski wanted me to stay on."

"Why?"

"Why do you think?"

"Why didn't you?"

"The only person who should have any real power over you is your girl. Other girls, guys, no matter how much you like them, forget it. Roman's a hell of a cat and I don't mind a scene like that if I'm the one who's running the number, but I ain't about to play the worker on hand for some other cat."

"What if you set it up right in your mind? What if you do it your way within someone else's context?"

"That kind of thinking applies sometimes, but not now. Here, it would just be a rationalization. You're a follower; you've lost control; you've lost the lead."

5. A girl of twenty; long, Indian-black hair; sea-water green eyes; smooth, tight skin. She's come west from New Hampshire, has settled in L.A., and has spent the past

year working for political-reform candidates—McCarthy, Bradley, Unruh. I meet her at the Whiskey, take her up to Jim's, swim with her. She's quick, graceful, affectionate, has a pretty smile (with one slight gap in the teeth), and a joyous laugh.

Jim's not in, but a group of BEU staff workers, six, have been working day and night for a week on a poverty program for the South. They are talking in the living room as we come in from the pool, and I introduce her briefly, catching nothing. Upstairs, we make love, a good, satisfying hour; then lie, rest, talk, wrestle with thumbs.

"Have you ever been with a spook?" The question is almost against my will. Still don't want to hear yes, while knowing, too, that yes, will maintain, increase, interest, and desire. She looks to be figuring an answer, pressing her memory, counting.

"You're the first *white* cat I've been with since I came to L.A. The second in my life."

It comes like a bomb, but I let it fizzle.

"How about some food? I'm starved."

She says spareribs wouldn't be bad, and I take off down the hill to cop; but, before, I turn at the bedroom door and say:

"Why don't you go in and say hello to the BEU guys. They're good."

It isn't until I have left, traveled, picked up the goods, driven halfway back, that I wonder where I will find her, doing what. A neatly laid plan.

The living room is empty, but there's noise upstairs, not from my room but from the bedroom next door. Wandering in, I see a lush mural, bodies disrobed, several hard black male forms, hers, seated, supine, curled, contorted. Laughter, smiles; grunts and moans of delight.

Her face is flushed, look glazed, wall-eyed. Can you *dig* it, New York, can you *dig* it? Again, I can; for I am reassured: when I permit myself to look, I gauge that I fall in all right, neither David nor Goliath. It holds its own okay. But wonder once more whether such concern, breaking here, no doubt, the membrane of obsession, isn't the special—hence, limited—province of youth, even youth deranged, whether ripening with age and experience won't yield, at best, tolerant amusement, indulgence with such folly or, at worst, impatience and scorn.

Is Byzantium necessarily the ultimate point at which the wise man disembarks? Is this world, J.B.'s, filtered through the prismatic consciousness of J.T., finally no more than another *scene*, its inclusiveness an illusion, its waters a mirage, its promises a deception? Are the sirens destined to static, shrillness, the trip only ostensibly free, a perilous price to be exacted as soon as bankruptcy has rendered one impotent to pay? Is this country, any country, no country for men?

Sure hope not, and believe not, too. Don't take the easy out, citing Mailer, Rojack, Shago Martin, N. T. Kingsley of Maidstone; think rather of the wisest fellow, Bellow, of aged Sammler, immigrant product, unique product at once of Bloomsbury and Cracow, of Wells and the Talmud, who is pinned, literally, up against the wall by a slick, sharp pickpocket of a spook whose presence, like "a law of nature," like "a stone falling, a gas rising," makes his heart sink:

There the man held Sammler against the wall with his forearm… unbuttoned himself. Sammler heard the zipper descend. Then the smoked glasses were removed from Sammler's face and dropped on the table. He was directed, silently, to look downward. The black man had opened his fly and taken out his penis. It was displayed to Sammler with great oval testicles, a large tan-and-purple uncircumcised thing—a tube, a snake; metallic hairs bristled at the thick base and the tip curled beyond the supporting, demonstrating hand, suggesting the fleshly mobility of an elephant's trunk...Over the forearm and fist that held him Sammler was required to gaze at this organ. No compulsion would have been necessary. He would in any case have looked...

A session, a lesson, a warning, an encounter, a transmission.

So I nurtured my interest, say yes to the vision, return with the girl to my room, feed her chicken and ribs, and fall off to happy sleep. She will come again.

6. A party, literally, of hundreds. It seems as though half of the Strip has been evacuated, landed at J.B.'s to swim and eat and dance and love.The nucleus, again, is the BEU; supposed to have been a celebration for them, thirty or forty, but there are the others, unknown, uninvited; many black football players as well—Willie Davis, Don Shy, Les Shy, Paul Warfield, Cookie Gilchrist, John Wooten, Jim Pace, O.J., and J.D., Boom-Boom, Timmy, LeRoy, Lenny, Jon.

It is during this evening that I have come fully to appreciate the house, friends, the life; come to understand that I have never before been so content, felt so right about people, pace, rhythm, mood; been so sure certain men—Jim, these—are, in a fundamental sense, the privileged, the elect.

About midnight, mist and chill having set in, I move up to my room for my leather jacket. Check; it's not in the closet. Wouldn't be exceptional, could think I'd left it elsewhere, somewhere, were it not that in the inside pocket of that jacket I had stashed seven hundred cash, all I had in L.A., and my return ticket to New York. On the floor of the closet is the airline envelope in which they had been folded, a grotesque taunt for the finale.

I sit trembling, enraged, on the end of my bed; bitter, then simply discouraged, sick with sadness, sad not only at the iconoclastic impact of the message the disappearance implies, at what it suggests about the easy inflations of fantasy, the pathos inherent in the longing for Utopia, but sad also at the sudden recognition of my own distance from the cleansing I had thought I had successfully passed through, from the sense of openness, receptivity I had hoped I'd already achieved: for some unsecreted bile, unemulsified fats, were exacting their price; unreformed suspicions running amuck—thieves, suck-scoundrels, *niggers* all.

Transformed abruptly into shame as J.B. comes in, hesitant in his own home: I didn't mean to disturb you. Are you working? No. No, just sitting. It's all been stolen. His face twists with pain: Oh my God, Toe, I'm sorry. That's awful. Just wait here. "The charm of knowledge would be small," says Nietzsche, "were it not that so much shame has to be overcome on the way to it."

Five minutes later Boom-Boom is up. How much? *How* much? You crazy, man, keeping that kind of money in a pocket? Never trust *nobody* with that much around. I was once robbed of five thousand. By a woman! And I caught her, too; but I never took it back and I never hurt her. Boom-Boom is gentle with ladies. Five thousand! But Boom-Boom can always get hold of bread when he needs it. Don't worry, Toback, we'll get it back for you.

Some shouts downstairs; will everyone please come

to the front door! Everyone. Now.

I make connections. J.B., personally, will search every pair of pants, every crotch and every pussy, until he finds the valuables pulled pusillanimously from the inviolate privacy of his own J.T.; will show everyone what counts, terrorize acquaintances and friends, imprison them, until the riddle is solved, the transgressor apprehended and whipped, confidence restored.

Descending, the intensity of my celebration is dulled, then cut, by emptiness, regret. I see a group, a mob, of black faces, many familiar, friendly, and now all will be accused, insulted, for—what?—a paltry thing, money, for me. *Hey, boy, it doesn't matter really. I mean I can always make it or win it back. No need for commotion.* Attention gained, I would double my loss to flee from it; isn't the kind I was looking for or needed, no.

"I've been asked by Jim Brown to make an announcement."

It is one of the BEU workers, standing in front of the door, blocking it, Jim nowhere in sight. "The place has become too crowded, and since this wasn't intended to be an open house to begin with, it would be appreciated if everyone not a member of BEU or a guest of a member cleared out. Everyone except BEU members and their guests, please, out!"

That's all.

Relief, then anger renewed. Nothing. No help. Boom-Boom comes over again, this time with J.D.

"Don't worry, Toback, we'll get the cat sooner or later."

"Condolences, New York," J.D. puts in. "But what's money to a jet *setter*? As long as his style's alive and his words are smokin' out sweet songs, the ladies will be there. Dig it."

An hour later, I run into Jim.

"Sorry about what happened, Toe," he says. "One motherfucker can mess up a whole nice thing."

I smile, say yeah, it's okay, doesn't mean shit, and mutter to myself about single rotten apples in every cart as I go off to bed, the edge sharpened again.

7. The door has opened. The girl with the sea-water green eyes I'd found at the Whiskey has come back, is with me, eating fruit, in the living room. Jim comes in with a girl he's met dancing, a tall girl with a mad smile, funny, nervous, choking laugh connotative of hysteria. We all sit, talk. She, giggling, tells me with my eyes its a giveaway, flat out, I'm insane. A freak claiming kinship. Maybe. Sometimes. At least, now.

Jim feels that call makes the mood; mumbling, leads us all into his room. Jim and his, I and mine, tandem. Isaac Hayes singing about his two women, a dark low room, a wide low long bed; all of us on it, naked. Mixed doubles. Mounting, I serve first, feel good, loose; sense no time passed, no disconnection, from the other night; sense her feeling the same. Feel the rhythm picked up on the other side, single to our double, double to our triple. The bed sways, swings, bounces, springs. Two become one, four become two, then four one; blending, melding. Black and white, female, male. I hold her, press her, taking her beat, giving her mine; throw ours to them, receive theirs. For the first time ever, as though in the beginning, discovering it, creating a form to be followed for ages, by ourselves again, by others after we are gone.

But know even then that the attribution of such dimension separates, isolates, one, a white American man, me.

See black; inexhaustible, dark, dangerous wells of motion and time and force, see it for a splendid moment purged of unfamiliar odors, discomforting hues, see it black-white, transcendent; but then see it, as before, as always, black.

Go back then, alone, to proof, display, victory. Like the other time, but the stakes higher now, the highest, J.B. And I begin to see that she knows it, too, not for nothing having made me the long-awaited, longed-for number two. She helps, working for herself and me, for him, pushing, driving, squeezing, blasting out all juices and fumes, a shuddering throb, finally; then rests, close to sleep. Can rest now, sleep only now, in satisfaction, drained—a moment of love, an obliteration of loneliness and terror, a war, a peace, a celebration, over.

That's Hollywood; that's showbiz.

Another Point of View

A group of fifty from the Black Student Union at UCLA, a large share athletes, came up to Jim's for advice, direction in their move to procure more palatable conditions, terms, prospects for themselves and for those who would succeed them. Balanced on his stereo cabinet, soaked in basketball sweat, Jim took charge, cutting off any who strayed from the line he was trying to pursue, encouraging, elaborating.

The only white face in the room, I looked to blend, unobtrusive, into the wall. Strange, new, dark faces. Felt, in odd sections, emanations of hostility, confusion; from others, curiosity. What, after all, the fuck was he—I—doing there? Jim felt them, too, anticipated my exit even as I was laying plans gracefully to make it, said:

"If anyone here still thinks that black people can only count on each other for improvement and change, I don't have any use for him, can't deal with him; cause it should be obvious that no matter what obstacles certain people may be putting in your way and no matter what narrowness they might display, other white cats are looking to work with you and are in full sympathy with your goals. You only waste time and hurt yourself if you turn them away, bickering within. Jim Toback over there, who's staying at the house with me, is a case in point. He's a writer and he backs up all the way. If you can't dig that, you'd better leave."

Grateful, warmed, flushed, I shuffled in place like an aging baseball player on his Day. What else could I have done? Three bows and arms raised above the head would have been good off-rhythm comic relief, but the crowd was too large; decided against it. I kept quiet, stared down.

Meeting adjourned, the crowd thinned; fifteen minutes later, all the students were gone, all except a thin, delicate man, bright black eyes; intense, nervous, obsessed, hands rubbing thighs, stomach; teeth sucking, biting lips. One is tempted to say "boy," for he couldn't have been much beyond his early twenties and looked some years younger. He had moved to a far corner of the room, back to the people leaving, waiting until they were gone.

Edging uneasily, irregularly, toward Jim, almost inaudibly he said, "Did you see the put-downs on you in *Soul* and *Jet?*"

Jim, voice pitched to match, stepped up next to him. "Which ones are you talking about?"

"The new ones. They're in the current issues. I was reading them today. The article in *Soul* said you were taking Tom roles in your movies, playing for white bread."

"*Who* said that?" The control was uncomfortable, forced.

"LeRoy Robinson."

"You *sure* about that?"

"I told you; I just read it today."

Still muzzled, all in tones close to a whisper. "I'm sorry; I can't believe LeRoy would have written that about me. He's been a good friend to me for years. He wouldn't attack without telling me he was going to."

"I read it. Today. That's what it said."

Jim's eyes narrowed. "You've got it wrong. Someone else may have said it. *He* didn't."

"Well—"

"Well what?"

"Maybe it *was* someone else, but I'm pretty sure."

Impatience now in J.B.'s face, voice, leaning on his antagonist. "I *know* it was someone else." His mouth started to spread, the barest suggestion of a smile. "That would be like *Toback* betraying me. Real friends don't pull that kind of shit on each other."

Turned, walked out to shower, dressed for the evening.

Alone with me, the other came over to the couch where I was seated, dropped down, said:

"You were embarrassed before, weren't you?"

"Yeah. I guess I was."

"Why?"

No reserve in the line I could feel him coming to follow, but his voice was still so soft I was, instinctively, open to giving him room to go on.

"Well..." Entrapped, I hesitated. One's reasons for evasion rarely transcend the borders of cowardice. So: "I suppose because I was conscious of being the only white cat in the room and knew that by calling the number of the people who felt hostile to me, Jim was protecting me, doing my job for me."

I waited.

"What are you doing out here?"

"Writing about Jim."

"What?"

"Well, what he's like, what he represents to black people, to America."

"What's that?"

"Well, it would seem to me he's your only potential hero; in some ways, the whole country's—black and white. On the surface, movies, sports, girls, businesses; beyond—decency, self-reliance, honesty in his relations with everyone; he's straighter than anyone I've ever met. A personification of American success, a dreamer of its dream, a possessor of that dream. He's assertive, articulate; moves, does; and with rhythm, boy [half smiled; got nothing in return]. All black cats can look up to him, learn from him, which is the first, essential quality a leader needs to have."

"You think that's what young black people are interested in? Sports? Movies? Money? Fucking off?"

The other's tone was still so winsomely gentle, affectionate, that I couldn't summon any resistance, sharpen any edge.

"Sure; it's hardly everything, but I wouldn't put them down as undesirables—black or white, young or old."

"You would be wrong."

Quite simple; flat, polite, uncompromising rejection. He waited. I waited, asked, finally what *he* did.

"I work for SNCC. I was their press secretary, wrote speeches for Rap. I'm a writer, like you."

"Why would I be wrong?"

"Because young black cats are getting hip and realizing that the important goals in life aren't fame and money and girls in a sick, unredeemable society, but involvement in activities that will demolish that society. If there isn't a complete structural reorganization, there's never going to be any real improvement in conditions for black people in this country, material or spiritual."

"What about the BEU? They're getting a lot of black cats into development of their talents and into finding skills—"

"Doesn't matter, Jim," the name uttered with warmth, placation for the interruption. "It isn't going to make a bit of difference. The institutions themselves, the competitive nature of the system, the assumptions about the limits of political and social possibility, all must go, and nothing but bullshit will happen until they do. Jim Brown doesn't hold a prayer as the real black hero. He's talented, he's smart, he's generous; but he's involved in old ideas and old solutions—partying, pleasure, competition, work—making a mark in what is always going to be a white world. Hip black cats won't ride with that anymore. Jim isn't politically imaginative enough to see what's needed. The times are passing him by. In fact, he isn't even political, he's private. He's individual instead of collective. His word just isn't ours."

Open with: Who wants a world whose emphasis is on the collective, which loosens the individual's spring, whether it's black or white? Then: You don't understand. You're off in every way. See first that Jim's not nearly so simple as you make him out. In working with whites and competing against them, he's growing into something larger himself and serving example to any black cats or white cats watching, indicating the surest, maybe only, way to satisfaction, to realization of energies that, finally, are all they have, all they can ever count on.

Say, too: Don't feel certain J.B. isn't looking to do more than you see, than he says now. A black ruler, a benevolent despot, not severed from, rather, transcendent of, the blood-mixing you deplore; that, perhaps, is where his energies, once realized, will carry him. One couldn't know now, the time's wrong today, and he'd make that move only, if ever, when it was right.

Reiterate: Now he's opening ends for black people, providing a field on which they can play out their longings, selves. And what America suffers from most deeply is an inability to create conditions for individuals to find precisely those openings. Would yours, or would it substitute obverse deceptions, evasions; even deny they should exist at all?

See beyond to personal analysis, understanding: Tight control of himself, of his own speed and intelligence and rage—muzzled, unleashed only at his will; that being power in its most difficult, again personal, form. From a back room, from servants' quarters, no matter how sweet, his mother a maid, he's moved to possession, his own, and will not part with it, won't believe others don't want the same, sees them disclaiming only when the odds are out. Or if the rejection is total, without condition, sees it as the denial of natural instinct, no symptoms of cultural disease.

Or take it up on my own account: Unless a white man is to renounce utterly, shadowing Tolstoy, all he has and, more, the very idea of possession he has inherited or assumed; unless he is willing to submit to a basic reconstitution of the content and order of his life, he can accept your vision only to the extent of his gluttony for humiliation and self-contempt.

Still, there was no end to the combinations and permutations of twists, perversities, necessarily inherent in any honest response; more, no way in which a white man, harboring even a residual claim to dignity or pride, could dispel outright the notion that, if black himself, his rage, his impulse to retribution, random, purgative violence, might pale by comparison the programmatic, constructive negations of a SNCC revolutionary. So, rhythm bollixed by his voice, unexpected presence, I didn't say it, any of it; hands low, setting him up, said instead:

"If you could move into this house right now, have all Jim's girls, money, deals; if you could run the BEU, earn the respect of all its members—would you take that in return for relinquishing your program, agree not to promote it or work for it or talk about it? Would you still believe in it?"

"It's very simple. You're asking if I'd rather make another, different country or have some of the fat from the corpse of this one."

"And—"

"No."

"Is that true of Rap? Stokely? All of the people in SNCC?"

"All that I know myself. But what did you mean by

girls? They're *women*. And to a *black* man, women means *black* women, to be treated monogamously, respectfully, reverently; because someday they may become mothers of future black warriors, brothers on the line."

Sex as pleasure, love; women as passion, battle, romance. No place in the Revolution, which, then, forget. But, again, didn't say it. Said nothing, waiting, and got a hand, a quiet good-bye.

Shortly, Jim came in.

"I like that cat," I heard myself say. "He's nice; he's smart."

J.B. looked down, coldly, said, "You asking me or telling me."

"Well, I liked him. I thought he was smart. I'm *telling* you."

"I know the cat a lot better than you do, and he's not 'nice' and he's not 'smart' in any honest way."

If he had had any hesitation in suspecting the revolutionary of attack and denigration, it had now been removed. And if he had entertained hope that his friend, his *capo*, would respond with forceful defenses and confutations, that, too, had gone. He tightened, glared; then looked away, down, and walked out.

In the morning, Jim cooked eggs and steak for both of us, said he'd like me to come to a motel later on where the BEU was meeting. He was planning to organize a poverty program, a new direction for the Union. I said I'd be glad to, was happy to find no bitterness from the night before.

On the way to the motel I bought a copy of *Soul*: one reference to Jim, hardly derogatory, and not in any article by LeRoy Robinson.

In the convention room: Curtis McClinton, Timmy Brown, Kelly, Warfield, Wooten; Ernie Thomas, for years a special assistant to King; staff workers; Paul Block (arranging, noting, providing; clearly more than an agent to J.B.; the only other white, his partner, his friend). All were young, close to, less than, J.B., strong, healthy; a clean-looking group.

"In the past, the BEU has specialized in assisting black people's efforts to get into areas they're prepared to compete in; or sometimes in training them so that they'll be prepared someday in the future."

Dressed in a dark-brown business suit, four buttons across the breast, snug, tie knotted tight, noose-like under the collar, he sat at the head of a rectangular table, voice pitched an octave lower than natural, leaning slightly forward on his chair; authoritative, mannered; feeling, playing out, his role in relation to the room.

"But today I want to introduce a new perspective into our work. I want to institute a program that starts with essentials—food and clothing. I've picked out the poorest county in Mississippi, and I want to see to it that we enable the people living there, many of them starving, more than half of them chronically unemployed, all of them aware only of the lowest level of subsistence, that we enable them to eat, to dress properly, to accept the basics as a given. Briefly, the order of events will run like this:

"During the next few weeks, I want all of you to return to your home cities, walk the streets, call on your friends, enlist any support you can find, to raise money and to collect food and clothing. Then, at your own expense, I want you all to travel to Holly Springs, where we'll meet, assort all the material contributions, talk with the people, and distribute the goods to them. But this will only be the beginning: the trouble with similar programs in the past has been that contact wasn't maintained. This time, designated BEU workers will remain down there and will begin job training, educational assistance, and voter registration as soon as the minimal point of health has been reached. Then we'll all return in nine months or so for renewal of contributions, and spread the program into other depressed counties all over the South.

"The reason I ask you to do all this on your own bread and your own time is that that way your involvement in it is bound to be greater than if it were simply a publicity tour or a pleasure trip. It has to be a sacrifice with no ulterior motives, only a sympathy for people far less fortunate than ourselves, people so badly off that they can't even begin to function on a level of equality, can't even begin to test themselves to see what they are or aren't capable of achieving.

"Now I'm aware that some of you may be afraid for your careers, so let me reassure you. This is an integrated county, about three-quarters black, and we'll be helping everyone, black and white. And it will have the sanction of established organs in this country: the Ford Foundation is going to help with a grant, and Javits may assist us in challenging the government to match whatever we come up with. So you don't have to worry about accusations or recriminations over 'black power,' 'black militance,' 'black separatism,' 'black racism,' or any of the other bullshit that lightweights like to throw out."

He waited. The room had been silent, attentive, say even transfixed. They were as large, duly successful—equals. They had found their way, but would listen, follow; for the trust, the respect, was absolute. The Gaylords—survived, softened, matured; with their man, their warlord, J.; each having found, served, the other's need.

"I know this isn't going to be easy for some of you." His voice relaxed. He could anticipate success. "You may have obligations to your family, your girl, your team, whatever. But it's important work, necessary work, and good work. And I've found that it can give a kind of personal satisfaction and happiness that just isn't available in any other way. So, if you do have trouble working out the time, come to me and we'll rap about it and see if there isn't some way it can't be handled. Just for a rough estimate, how many of you can commit yourselves now?"

Everyone raised his hand. "Beautiful. I really appreciate this. Now just let me identify you individually in case you're not all familiar with each other."

Gave brief sketches, background, and credentials, came to me, said, "Jim Toback is a writer from New York, a close friend of mine and a supporter of the work we're trying to do. He's willing to help out in speech writing, releases, whatever comes up: the important thing is, no matter what, he's with us a hundred percent."

A *hundred* on the nose; a Gaylord, and it made me feel good, a fine respite from the need to fight, conquer, prove, as if these words, that phrase, that hundred percent were, finally, what I had come to that motel that day, to L.A. that month and the time before, to hear. *You outta caps; far away from himself, white.* They were only slogans now, the sting gone from the mockery, comic relief to check my embarrassment at the public salute; for I knew now and was *glad* to know, that J.B. was not bored with the business of the BEU, not simply a goof of a freak, a steel blade in a black sheath, not just rhythmic but off-rhythmic; not simply, not at all, the jive-ass nigger I had hated others for believing him, all of *them*, to be, had hated *myself* for believing them, him, to be; but rather a man, affectingly uncertain, disciplined, hard-working, whipped on by an inviolable vision of dignity and by the promises of desire.

There were few men in America I was more interested in meeting than Bill Russell. I had been a Celtic fan from the early Cousy-Sharman years, but grew obsessed in the late fifties as Russell, close to seven feet, stalking whole teams defensively with his terrifying, ebony, chisel-bearded face and tentacular arms, took control of the club and sport in which I harbored my own athletic ambitions. Following a Russell-Celtic adventure over a season was like watching a Western serial or reading a progression of spy novels in which, threatening appearances baldly to the contrary, one knew one's side (the *right* side) ultimately would win. The emphasis, the angle of curiosity, was on means rather than ineluctable ends; which evil force—Wilt, Pettit, or Baylor and West—would be denied entrance into the hole of power blocked by Russell and his gang? With what moves? In how many games? From what gross deficits and disadvantages?

George Plimpton, who had traveled with the Celtics in 1969 to write a book about basketball, whetted the edge, assured me that Russell was one of the most imposing men he had ever encountered, brilliant to the point of intimidation. And there was Jim, scrupulous in the objects of his praise, who had often mentioned Russell in tones and contexts of uniquely unqualified respect; as a man of intelligence and courage, conceivably the most important and most successful black athlete ever, a relentless, determined winner.

So, one afternoon, when Jim suggested that I accompany Russell and him on a round of golf, I was elated, stipulating only, for the sake of my honor and their patience, that I walk along rather than play. While we were waiting for Russell to pick us up, Fred Williamson came by, was invited to join, agreed. He is a slick, mannered, imitative approximation of J.B., a former cornerback for the Chiefs whose reputation in karate and sense of self-advertisement had caused *Life* to do a story on him the week before the first Super Bowl, an article suggesting, boasting, that it might well be the lethal hitting of "the Hammer" (as he was then called) that would determine the outcome of the game. Flattened by a straight-arm or a knee from Donny Anderson ten minutes into the fourth quarter of the Green Bay victory, the Hammer had to be helped off the field. Out of football, into Hollywood, he was getting on in the movies now and in television; he was an agency's, a producer's, dream of a spook—strong, clean, handsome, graceful, glib. His pants were cut like Jim's, shaped tight to the contours of his buttocks and thighs, shirt stretched across the hard curves of shoulders and chest. The walk, too, like Jim's, contained traces of a limp, yielding the impression of awesome reservoirs of force and speed, held skillfully in control. There was, finally, something that forced one to reserve affection, an unnaturalness, a façade, a pressed laugh, a smile flashed too easily and too well, a look unfocused, on the run, from one object, person, to another, never taking, never seizing; too much of "this bitch from last night" and "that bitch from the night before," too strenuous an effort to appear confident, uncomplicated, sure.

Analysis, however, is here no more than a mode of implementation, a substantiation of judgment already rendered, instinctively, before. And that judgment was not mine of him, but my intuition of his of me. For the first time with any of J.B.'s good friends, I felt no emanations of warmth, interest, concern. Or even wonder. Ignored. One hundred percent cut to ninety-five.

Russell arrived, and one's worries over brotherhood with Gaylords and bloods were suspended. For the proximity of his physical presence, the informality, the opportunity, suddenly, simply, to watch and to learn, the awareness of the two athletes, competitors, J.B. and Russ, who had informed the masculine fantasy life of the nation, jolted me into the assumption of a new role: spectator, student, referee. The impressions were clear, short, consecutive; a contact sheet: quick, black, aggressive, curious eyes; hard, finely shaped lips, a gap in the upper row of teeth; a fast, enraptured, spontaneous smile, cracked open into a hysterical laugh, a bellowing, mad howl, the long neck taut, muscles rippling around the Adam's apple; sharp, pointed, bearded jaw; flat, broad granite chest and shoulders, squared, long, stretched muscles in the stomach, legs; great, hooked, beaklike arms; long, nervous fingers. Made me feel, standing next to him, looking up, not so much short as boyish, small. Made, finally, even Jim seemed scaled down a cut, as though serving notice of a new, superior physical breed of man for another epoch, or the return of one past. A *monster*.

It was close to the start of a new season, the first for more than a decade in which Russell would not be part of, dominating, the league; joining Jim as an entry, the only heroes of modern sport who had quit at their peak, who would afford no view, not even a cameo, of decline, to friends, enemies, themselves. There had been talk of his following Jim into movies or Ali into lecture tours of colleges and universities; but now, driving out to the course, his mind was on basketball.

"Auerbach has to be the best coach who ever lived; in *any* sport. No one's ever had so many winners, no one's ever had such control of his guys, the kind of absolute respect of everyone who dealt with him."

He waited, took the silence as objection, or at least question.

"You've got to agree, right? I mean, even more than Lombardi, the cat has to be the strongest winner who ever coached. Not even Lombardi, right?"

"I didn't say nothin' about Lombardi," Williamson said. "I'll believe what you say."

It passes coincidence that the obsession with competition and victory is most obviously, most immediately apparent in the two athletes, Brown and Russell, whose devotion to success in games and struggle, whose religious identity of good with it, was the unique creator of self. For without such devotion, without an insistence on winning of such single-minded ferocity, without, by extension, such terror of failure and defeat, what move from where he began, what mark, what claim, what projection, what growth could either have made? Other running backs had Brown's strength and speed, other centers Russell's height and dexterity; so talent being even or close, the best would have to pluck his prize with his wit and his will. Take it back further, before high school, take it to Manhasset for J.B., to Oakland for Russ, seeds planted but trees not yet grown; how does a Gaylord become a warlord, his blade a sword; how a mean boy hard, a tough one strong; how does cockiness ripen into confidence, greed mellow to hunger, bitterness blossom into rage; how, finally, does a boo-boo become black if not by transforming his instinctive understanding of America's profoundest needs and values and rewards into a daily, perpetual quest for the cultivation and demonstration of the limits of his rhythm and power? To choose one's class and field and to measure one's possibilities against others in them and, then, against oneself; to resist the temptation to relaxation and ease, to compel oneself to strictness in the pursuit of one's broadest reach, is to settle into the only mode of attack from which protection from despair becomes possible.

Bill Kelley, a black track star at Fieldston, the high school I was going to six years after his graduation, went on to Harvard, started writing stories and novels, and soon became one of the finest black writers in America. When the school newspaper did an interview with him and asked what teacher had helped most to make him good, the anticipation was that he would say Archibald MacLeish, his Harvard mentor, and the hope was that he would mention Elbert Lenrow, his Fieldston English man. Smitty, he said. Alton Smith, the Fieldston track coach. "When I was putting the shot for him he made me understand two things: that I had to win, and that I had to better myself by at least an inch on each new attempt. Without that attitude, I'd never have done anything worthwhile in any area. I'd never have grown."

If, then, Russell and Brown had tapped out on themselves, if they had agreed to live by calculated gambles, and had both of them won a remarkable share of their wagers, and if everything they had become was the sum of the stakes they had played for and achieved, the habit of being in action and of caring passionately for the outcome had hardened into permanence. No Celtic "6" or Brown "32" needed to be on either back for competition to attain the condition of combat, or victory the dimension of salvation. They agreed on fifty dollars for the match before them now, but it would be a token, a trophy: booty in metaphor.

As we pulled in at the club, Jim started his laugh, a low chuckle first, shoulders bouncing, a giggle, then a rumble, a roar.

"What you goin' on about, Mr. Brown?" Russell asked.

"I was just thinking, it's a wonder this car didn't collapse from the sheer weight of egos. We got the four biggest egos in America all locked up in the same machine."

Although he has only been playing a few years, Brown shoots regularly in the low seventies, considerably better than Russell, so a stroke-a-hole spot was accorded. The early holes were played at a relaxed pace, ease an unarticulated convention, a prelude to the edges ahead. Jim was stopped by several sons and fathers, signed autographs; Russell, too, but, looking straight ahead, he said no, didn't do that. No one asked Freddy or me.

Freddy, his son of seven living with his former wife, said, "Advice is essentially bullshit. If you're asked for it, give it, but with modesty and the understanding that you can't ever get fully into anyone else's head, even your own boy's. Everyone has to make his own decisions about his own life. Never force it on anyone. You've got to be there until the kid's six or so, but after that, he should be on his own to a great extent. All he needs from his father is to know that if he's needed, he'll be there. Even if you could make your kid over in your own image, you shouldn't; but you can't, so it don't make sense even trying. He's got to become what *he* is, and he will anyway, no matter what you tell him or do."

"That's the smartest thing I ever heard you say, Freddy," said J.B.

On the fifth hole, Freddy ripped the rear seam of his pants. His shirt sleeves were short, too short to tie around his waist for cover, and he asked me for mine (a pink silk with french cuffs) in trade; I agreed. Chest bare, black muscles glittering, my silk an apron for his ass, he continued to play; and I, his damp shirt too large, loose on my back, feeling, oddly, good with it, jive-ass or no, a brother, a spook.

Jim had moved a few strokes ahead, but on the fourteenth hole Russell, red tee grooved through the front of his hair, jerking, a crazy laugh resonating across the fairways, bunkers, ponds, began to work his whammy, using me, white warlock, as his agent; before each shot, would tell—loud, for J.B. to hear—me precisely what he was about to do. *Gonna hook this sucker onto that green ten feet to the left of the pin; gonna put this fifty footer two feet short, then tap it in;* and did it.

By the eighteenth, given the stroke-a-hole odds, Russell had drawn to a tie. Jim suggested doubling the wager, got Russell's laugh and affirmation. The sun was setting, breeze had stirred to wind, and although the sense of good feeling was still there, the tension, suddenly, was unmistakable; as though by design, the competition had come distilled to this one last hole for resolution, a moment for crystallization. Compressed further when Brown landed on the green in three, Russell in four; Russell lay forty feet beyond the pin, Jim twenty feet to the left of it, level.

"No way I'm gonna miss this putt; you know that, Toback, don't you?"

I nodded, smiled, wondered, assumed against reason, yes; I do know it. J.B., grinning, winked at me, edged up behind Russell as he prepared his stroke, threw his shadow heavily across the path to the hole.

"I'm gonna psych the sucker," he whispered.

But Russell was off on his own, unhinged from any

thought, possibility, consideration save the scent of his own victory. He was braced under the basket to block Hal Greer's twenty-foot jump shot on its upward arc, to steal the dribble off Baylor's drive, to edge Wilt off the board, clutching the loose ball off the rim and, in one motion, flinging it downcourt to a hanging Howell. He didn't see the shadow: hunched, hitched, hit through, watched the ball roll, hop, curve, drop.

And then it came—a triumphant, howling shriek of a laugh, a laugh more maniacal, less controlled, than J.B.'s; easily as remarkable. "There's nothing," says Belloc, "worth the wear of winning, but laughter and the love of friends."

"Lawdy, Lawdy!" cried Jim, shaking his head.

"Ain't the Lord that's smokin' your ass," yelled Russell through his laugh; "it's me!"

Jim, uncharacteristically, spent several moments measuring his putt, analyzing all its angles, gauging the roll; then stroked, firmly, evenly, through the ball, watching it edge, rim the cup, fall dead two inches away.

Strangely, it was still as though I'd never seen him lose, still impeccably the warlord of all warlords; for Russell, slouching as we walked to the clubhouse, looked once more like the member of another species, gigantic, unreachable, extrahuman, his club a miniature wand.

"Hey, William," Jim said to him, smiling, tapping him on the arm, "that's the last time I spot you a stroke a hole, boy."

The End of Competition

Jim went back to work on tennis, advancing each day roughly as much as an ordinary athlete fresh on taking up the game would have progressed in a month. After one late night, a long party, he asked, challenging, if I would be ready to play early in the morning, say nine. We would both sleep a few hours, then go off. I said, had to say, okay, but as I lay in bed, restive, wasting a fair share of the alloted time, I couldn't overcome the suspicion that this next would be our first, last, and only real match. For if until that moment I had experience and background in my favor, one day more and the upper hand would pass to him. In all athletic rivalries there is that instant, remarkably precise and unmistakable to both parties, when the shift in odds takes place, when the favorite becomes the dog and knows that from then on he will remain the dog, winning only infrequently and by the whims of chance. It was a fair supposition that similar thoughts were taking hold in J.B.'s mind, also sleepless, at the same time.

So for this day alone we would be equal, and my need to win would be its most intense, for it would be my last shot, my sole opportunity to earn one of those rare moments of grace which memory would be able to recall happily, at will. And for J.B., in contrast, if ever his blade were to want honing, it would be now; a loss would exact its smallest price, for the point had been reached, and if his string of victories did not start that day, it would the next.

I can't remember at any other time in Hollywood with Jim, feeling precisely the kind of uneasiness I felt that morning, that ride to the court, that match. The fatigue, the anticipation, the yearning, the dread, weighed heavily enough that even now, in the tranquillity of recollection, I cannot focus the sequential details of the event, only the loaded climaxes that lent it form.

Anxious over the danger of falling behind, sensing that early domination would suggest to us both that I did have this one last match coming before roles were reversed, I played the first set as though it were the last; charging drop shots that were out-bet winners, chasing back lobs into the wire fence behind the base line, pursuing crosscourt drives in the hope of pushing back any kind of return. Jim was relaxed, warming up, using the set for pace; I lost only a game.

We had rented the court for two hours and had agreed on a token sum for the winner. It occurred to me as we were playing the second set that the time limit might cause confusion if the sets were even and the games in the odd set favored one over the other, but I said nothing, didn't look to clear it up. I was more concerned with the cracks that had started to weaken my own game and with the sureness and control with which Jim was returning everything I offered. I was overrunning, misjudging, hitting wild and wide, volleying short, smashing long; as he, imperiously, glided, stroking, waiting for me to err.

Cocksucker! Motherfucker! Worthless, rotten, lowlife prick! One had never been renowned for the richness or variety of one's vocabulary during the desperate periods of athletic war. As physical complement, one's racket was hurled freely in several directions, ultimately (if unintentionally) across the net, barely by J.B.'s head.

"That's it," he said quietly, and started off the court.

"What do you mean?" I said, knowing, following. He turned around, faced me, a few feet away.

"I just can't play like that, balls flying all over the court, rackets coming at me. It messes up my game and it robs it of all the fun. Also (he leaned in, almost whispering, motioned to an older couple playing on the court behind us) it's not right to swear like that with those people around; you shouldn't be imposing your thing on someone you don't have a thing to do with. Why offend them? There's just no reason for it."

None indeed. One had suffered a lapse, characteristic to be sure, but fortunately checked—and by a boo, too, n.b. *that*—for informality was no license to rudeness; and, traditional aristocratic practice and assumption to the contrary, manners cease to serve even aesthetic functions when uninformed by consideration. Also, I wanted to get on with the match, to reach a decision, to work to the point where I knew, either way, who had won. Apologetically:

"It's out of my system. No more. Let's play."

We did, and Jim ran out the second set easily, and then, with some difficulty, the third. Close to panic, the odor of defeat jolted me into better form for the fourth; came back to take it, Jim seeming, suddenly, tired, letting up. In the fifth we were tied at one when the two-hour period closed; but the proprietor came out to wave us on, his next entry having just canceled.

"What do you want to do?" Jim said.

"What do you mean? Finish!"

"Finish what?"

"This *set*, the match."

He shrugged.

"Three out of five, right?"

He didn't answer, moved into the net, glowering at me across it, the racket a paddle in his hand.

"I mean, we've split the first four sets and we're even here, so let's play it out and whoever takes it wins the match. Three out of five."

If my voice hadn't been raised a full octave, it was at least on the dominant; for I had never seen him in such rage—betrayed in the coiled tension of his muscles, the forced lock of his jaw. When he finally spoke, it was as a ventriloquist, the lips hardly parting, the tone muzzled, muffled, the projection bizarre; a strange, intimidating persona I was meeting now for the first time.

"Look, how many times have we played?"

"I don't know exactly. Quite a few but—"

And how many times have we played three out of five?"

"None, but—"

"And how many times have we played two out of three?"

"Always, but—hey, look, J. I'm not trying to beat you out of anything, but I figured that since it's two all in sets and since we can have the court for another hour, we might as well play it out."

Nothing, black on black. But the fear loosened, vanished. Feeling stronger, uncowed at least, I could offer, "Look, if you want to call it your match in two out of three, it's all right with me."

And we were back, consciousness regained after nightmare; the biceps, forearms, thighs relaxed; the racket dropped; the jaw opened, moved with the voice, louder, gentler.

"Hell no, Toe. But I paced myself for two out of three. I don't know anything about three out of five. It's a whole different thing."

He waited. I waited for him.

He said, "Okay, let's go."

He hit out, played the set as if in practice; and I played for all the balls, knowing then (particularly then, after the dispute, the revelation of anger, his, and terror, mine, the reminder that, finally, behind all the wit and whammy and countermoves was the primal, obvious reality of his incredible strength) that this was to be my last certain victory. I won, and felt no bitterness from him, no suggestion that we ought to have quit when the time was up, only a smile, compliments, congratulations, money. But they were misplaced. Gears had shifted for good in the last game.

Law and Order

I woke up one morning around eleven, came into the kitchen, and found Cookie Gilchrist leaning on the refrigerator, whispering into the telephone on the wall. Gilchrist is an oversized version of Jim—massive, black muscle; light, slow movements; a devastating running back in his prime whose conflicts with coaches and owners cut several years and dimensions of recognition from his career. Jim, in whose charge he has worked as a BEU organizer of athletic programs, is at once a noble and a bitter reminder to him of what he believes he should, could, would have become, had only his luck been better, had only he come along when it was possible to maintain one's integrity, to hold firm to one's image of manhood as a black man while succeeding within the system. I mixed some Ovaltine, waited for him to finish; when he did, asked where Jim might be.

"In jail."

There was a soft, slow quality in the voice, in the huge body as it rested back on the side of the sink; a reticence, a resignation suggesting that once again, unjustly, *they* had fucked *us* up, ten inches of spurred boot up our ass; a reserve suggestion further that I, J.T., was by no certain measure not one of *them* myself, or at least somehow in league with them, closer to them than to *us*. Which supposition (astute? misguided?) hurt, angered, me, for I was, indeed, shaken, enraged.

"In jail! What the hell for?"

"There was a traffic accident last week. Nothing big. A scrape. Jim agreed to show up in court this morning, but then they busted him last night. Out of nowhere. He's just cruising around with a chick and they stop him, cuff him, and lock him up."

"When will he be out?"

"Today; but the fucking hassle! The lowness of it! The humiliation they want to put on you."

"Who's *they?*"

Gilchrist smiled. "They" *were* all of "us"; they *were* J.T. But he said instead, "The sheriff. The guy has a vendetta going against Jim."

"Why? What for?"

Again the smile. "Supposedly, Jim said he was a racist over the radio a few years ago. But the real reason's that— fuck it, *you* know what the reason is. White folks will let you do anything you please as long as you show gratitude. You can make bread and play and party and get your name plastered all over the butt of this country, but you better be thankful for it, boy, and you better let 'em *know* you're thankful. Jim's attitude has always been he's got comin' what he's worked for, same as anyone who wants his ass licked in return has. He don't hide a thing. He ain't ashamed. He's one black man ain't about to be cowed by *nobody.*"

Gilchrist's voice was still soft, connotations of rehearsal in the rhythm of his words. It was a fair bet he had thought, said, the same of himself.

"But what about the power and the bread behind Jim? How can they keep getting away with it?"

"Getting away with what? They don't get him *convicted.* They just arrest him and charge him. Then at the trial it's thrown out as bullshit and Jim's off. But in the meantime it's the arrests that get all the publicity and attention, while the release and the exposure of lies and setups don't get heard of anywhere. Most cats in Jim's place would have gone on television long ago or called a press conference and laid it out directly, but Jim's not the kind to go justifying and explaining and excusing, especially when he didn't do nothin' in the first place except get framed. It would go against the whole idea of himself."

The surprise of the news had worn off, and I was now simply disgusted, longing so intensely for some kind of retribution that I wondered whether the exhilaration that accompanies pure anger wasn't here tied to a sense of joy that at last there was someone at whom my hatred could be directed, an excuse to strike out at a tangible, exaggerated, perverse reflection of my own, lately discovered, imbalances, an ultimate expiation of them.

"I know," I said. "But it's not likely that the sheriff is smart enough to understand a vision of self so complicated or so principled. So how does he know he's not going to be exposed? How can he take one dumb gamble after another and avoid eventually getting hurt?"

"Maybe he'll get it this time," Gilchrist said. "Maybe Jim will come back at him now."

"I hope so," I said, and dressed and drove down the hill for the newspapers to learn how it would be reported. On Sunset, a small Negro boy, soft round cheeks and a happy bounce in the balls of his feet, was carrying, selling, Herald-Examiners.

"Jim Brown locked up! Jim Brown locked up! Read about it; Jim Brown locked up!"

"Hey, give me a few," I said through the window.

He came over, dropped them on the seat.

"Why are you yelling that out so happily?"

He shrugged; shy, suspicious.

"Don't you like Jim?"

The boy looked at me, trusted.

"Sure I likes him. He's a hero, boy. But it sells a lot of papers. People likes to read about him like this because he's a idol."

"I guess so." I was oddly disappointed. Felt somehow Jim was being badly let down. I didn't like the little boy with the sweet face and started the car.

"Hey," he called in, his arms hanging through so I wouldn't go. "You just watch. Jim Brown gonna beat it. He always beat it. He gonna whip their ass, boy. He got pride."

"How do you know about pride so soon?"

"I know about it," he said; then with remarkably appropriate timing, pushed off a turn and went back to his beat, shouting "Jim Brown locked up!"

If a nine-year-old boo-boo had an instinct for what would make newspapers sell, Hearst's heroes surely knew no less. JAIL ACTOR JIM BROWN was blocked in bold print as the front-page headline. Below, the kicker ran "Jim Brown Released on Bail in Hit and Run." I pulled over to the curb and read the story:

Former football star Jim Brown spent the night in jail and appeared in court this morning to answer charges stemming from a traffic accident Friday in which a motorist claims he was assaulted.

He was released on $2000 bail in Beverly Hills Municipal Court and ordered to return to court August 28 for a preliminary hearing on a charge of felonious assault. He was also charged with two misdemeanors, hit-run driving and leaving the scene of an accident, and battery.

The athlete, now an actor, is accused of shoving Arthur Brush, 52, off the hood of Brown's car, where he had taken refuge following the accident. Brush claimed his arm was injured.

The former Cleveland Browns fullback was recognized last night by sheriff's deputies as they passed a car in which he was sitting with Miss Candy Kesner, 19, of 927 N. San Vicente Blvd., where the auto was parked. Deputies said the car belonged to Brown's roommate, Cookie Gilchrist, former Denver Broncos football player.

He was arrested on a warrant and jailed at West Hollywood sheriff's station.

Brush told deputies he was stopped in traffic behind a stalled car Friday at Santa Monica and La Ceinega Boulevards when a car struck his from the rear. He said he got out and showed the driver his license and asked to see the other driver's, but the driver refused.

Brush said the driver then attempted to drive off, but Brush was in front of the auto and leaped to the hood to avoid being struck. Some 75 feet further on, the driver leaped out and shoved Brush off the hood, he said. He managed to get a license number from the car, and deputies traced it to Brown.

Brown pleaded no contest last year on charges of assaulting a deputy sheriff who went to his apartment to investigate circumstances surrounding injury to actress-model Eva de Bohn-Chin. He was fined $500.

Deputy John Texeira, one of the two deputies involved in the earlier assault case, was one of the two deputies who recognized Brown last night and arrested him.

It was an out bet that the common response to the article would combine corroborated negative expectation and indignation with uncomfortable awe over relentless black brutality. Would there be no end to the trouble the boo would seek and find? Was there no boundary to his unreasoned hatred of whites?

And yet, short of assuming that public reaction was founded on the insight of a moth, one had to believe that some people, at least, would have serious reservations, would wonder whether the reporter's efforts at research and induction might not be wanting somewhat in rigor.

Who seeks safety on the hood of someone else's car, particularly when the driver of that car is presumably bent on murder? Even granting the impulsive acrobatics as an act of desperate self-preservation, by what supernatural dimensions of optical power can a man, transported unwillingly for seventy-five feet atop a speeding vehicle, be hurled from the vehicle and still catch, out of the corner of his eye, the precise sequence of a multidigit license number? More, by what miracle of coincidence does a casually passing deputy recognize a refugee from the law who is sitting in a rented car on a dark street in the middle of the night? And by what further leap into the occult does that roaming deputy, of all the deputies in Los Angeles County, turn out to be the very one whom the refugee had been charged with assaulting a year earlier? Indeed, why was apprehension of the refugee suddenly so essential in the first place, when he had been living openly at home, appearing freely in public throughout the week since his accident?

Barring, however, a special interest in the subject, one wouldn't ordinarily spend one's time performing an *analyse du texte* on Hearst stories. (What questions would I have asked a year before, when Jim was no more than a composite of exactly such headlines and such articles?) Perhaps it would constitute neither neglect nor simple-mindedness to any embarrassing degree if no suspicions at all were formed. Besides, the impact of the page issued not from the words on it but rather from the accompanying photograph, a UPI classic, showing Brown, black pants, black dashiki, black face, eyes close to shut, leading a chain gang out of a sheriff's bus, left wrist cuffed to the right wrist of a young white prisoner, whose left in turn is hooked to the right of another's, and so on down the line of five. Jim's mouth is tight, head hung in humiliation, a deputy with the crew cut of a convict watching with intensity from behind, his hand clutching the gun on his hip and what I want to know is how do you like your dark-eyed hero Mister Spook?

Back at the house, Scotty and Jeff, Cookie's sons, were shooting baskets. Scott's about nine, younger than his brother by a couple of years, but is the more aggressive, unabashedly curious, of the two. He is also—unlike his brother, who is already handsome in a romantic way-outrageously funny-looking, cute, with plump cheeks and a constantly beaming smile. If shown even the suggestion of affection or concern he will eagerly offer in exchange a complete revelation of everything on his mind.

"Did you see Mr. Brown today?"

"Not yet," I said.

He left his game, clasped his arms around my thigh, cheek snug, looking up. Jeff continued to play, but in slow motion, noiselessly, to listen without appearing to.

"Is he really in jail?"

"I don't know."

"That's what the newspaper said. I saw it. And I saw a picture of Mr. Brown right on the corner with handcuffs on his hands."

"Well, then, I guess he is," I said. "But he'll probably be out today."

"I hope so. Jeffrey cried when he saw the picture."

"I did *not*," Jeff said, humiliated, his back to us. "I did *not* cry."

"You did so," Scotty said. "I saw you. But that's okay. I did, too. You just didn't see me."

I headed into the house. Scotty called after me.

"You don't think he *did* it, do you?"

"Did what?"

"What he's in jail for."

"No, I know he didn't."

"They why did they put him in?"

"They don't like him," I said. Then, heading off the obvious question: "But you do, don't you?"

"Yes."

I skipped through the house, out the other side, dived into the pool, and—clouting the water in butterfly rage—played with the idea of wreaking some kind of revenge, drawing Jim into a decision to retaliate. Fight back together. I even had visions of physical combat, Jim and me against the sheriff and a group of deputies, hand to hand; then a shoot-out, Scotty and Jeff scuttling around pointing out locations, we picking them off onetwothree-fourfivepigeons just like that.

But when Jim returned, there was no gun, no scowl, not even an angry word. Only smiles, jokes with Scotty and Jeff, talk of tennis, plans for partying that night. And one ought, really, to have known; for to come back at that moment with excuses, explanations, retribution, would have been to admit—to me, to himself—that they had his number now, that this time they had got to him, dragged him to the level of their own pettiness and corrupted games and so beaten him. No, he would wait; first he would laugh, his laugh, and invite every friend and partner in Holly*wood*, Boom-Boom and J.D., Timmy and Bill, Leonard, Fred, and Jon, to serve notice to them, in case there was any doubt, that no bullshit thrown at him to shame him, to break his rhythm, to do him in once and forever so that none of them could look to him again with the same respect and the same hope, had even begun to work.

Only then, only after that release, only when the dead weight and dreariness of accusation had been lightened, balanced, obliterated with celebration and joy, only the next day would he make his move.

I was lying by the pool, and he came over quietly, joined me, waited several minutes, then said (hesitantly, shyly), "Hey, Toe, I'd like you to do me a *favor*." It occurred to me that, incredibly, this was the first time since I had known him that I had heard him use that word, the first time—after flying from London to see if he could help out with Mimi; after opening home, friends, new styles, himself, to me—that he had ever asked for anything himself.

"Absolutely," I cried, jumping up, failing to contain my excitement. "Anything at all."

"I'm going to lay out a thing to you, Toe: what went on with this charge and arrest and also some of the stuff from the past that led up to it, the balcony-throwing bullshit, the murder raps, the beatings, and all the rest. 'Cause this time they're setting it up to kill me, see, and the fact that I'm ready to die whenever it has to be, that I don't count on no one day being followed by the next, doesn't mean that I should lay on my butt and play along as the object of their insanity. They're just not going to stop this shit until I scare them a little and show them I ain't letting it go on forever. So what I'd like you to do is listen to what I tell you and then put it down in the form of a press release. I'm going to come out with some of it on television—Joey Bishop and Regis Philbin and whatever else I can work out; but I'd like to send it off with a release."

"You're down," I said. "I'm ready whenever you are."

Finally, I was happy not at the prospect of competition, at the opportunity to beat J.B. at a game, to measure myself against the strongest force I could find with an eye to cultivating, enlarging in the process; but rather at the chance simply to help him, and for no reason other than that I cared for him and admired him as a man and as a friend.

I listened, took notes, checked them with him, then

wrote; and in writing, felt first uncomfortable, strange, then exhausted. For in the movements and modifications of self, it is an art of no small significance to slip into, adopt, become another, if only for an hour, if only in the confines of a journalistic statement. To do so—to assume the voice of a separate being and to accept as one's own his experience, his longings and his fears—is to forge an irrevocable union, to enter into a compact that passes shares of each one's existence to the other, a conjunction of selves.

The result, distilled, reordered, is yet a direct transmission of Brown's revelation:

On Tuesday night, August 5, I was arrested by the sheriff's office of Los Angeles County and charged on three counts: two misdemeanors and a felony. In spite of willful deception and gross factual misrepresentation in the sheriff's office release to the media, I might have remained silent and contented myself with settlement in court. But this is only the latest in an apparently endless series of such bizarre episodes, and, as a result, I have decided finally to set the record straight. I wish to indulge in no counteraccusations, name-calling, or self-pity. I am not seeking to give the "other side" of the story. Nor will I try to explain anyone's motivations. I intend simply to relate a body of connected factual materials from which each may feel free to draw his own conclusions.

Over a year ago, when living in an apartment at 1010 North Palm Avenue, I was visited nearly every night for a period of two months by sheriff's deputies with warnings to keep my record player low. On one occasion I was informed that no one was supposed to be in my apartment, and ordered to produce identification. Only after I called the landlord would the deputies agree to leave.

If such attention to my personal life suggested future

trouble, I didn't have long to wait. After an argument with my girlfriend, Eva Bohn-Chin, and an accident in which Miss Chin fell from the balcony, the sheriff's office informed the press and thereby the American public that Miss Chin had charged me with assault with intent to kill. In reality Miss Chin never pressed any charges of any kind whatever. The charge came directly and solely from the sheriff's office itself. In fact Miss Chin *resisted* a full week of persistent attempts by sheriff's officers to induce her to lodge the very charges that they had publicly claimed she had already lodged. When she remained adamant in her refusal, the sheriff's office was forced to back down, asserting that Miss Chin had decided to "drop" her charges. As compensation, they then issued their own, claiming first that I had *pushed* a deputy, then that I had *hit* a deputy and, in a third and final version, that I had *interfered* with a deputy in the line of duty. The first two of these assertions were totally false, the third true only in the sense that I did not want to let the deputies into my apartment.

If the incident concerning Miss Chin violated the truth, the latest accusation insulted it. On the evening of Friday, August 1, I was driving my car on La Ceinega. Seated with me in the front was Bill Russell, the basketball player and coach. Another car, trying to get on the road, cut in front of me. I applied my brakes but the other car continued, grazing its left side against the right side of my front bumper. The scratch that it sustained, which was negligible, was caused by its own forward motion against my stationary vehicle. The driver of the car, Arthur Brush, and I both got out and exchanged relevant information, including name, address, and license number. Mr. Brush wrote it all down on a brown paper bag which he had withdrawn from the back seat of his car. I then told Mr. Brush that I was in a hurry and that insurance agents could settle the minor damages. When I returned behind my wheel, Mr. Brush seated himself on the hood of my car. I ordered him to get off, and when he refused I pulled off La Ceinega onto a side street where I again directed him to alight. He refused a second time, and I reacted by getting out and pulling him off by the arm. I then drove away with Mr. Russell. The three claims that Mr. Brush subsequently made: that my car ran into his car, that I hit him bodily with my car, and that I threw him to the ground are all equally secure in the realm of fantasy.

The following day the Highway Patrol reached my attorney, Mr. Richard Covey, and discussed the question of insurance forms with him. Nothing was said about charges of any kind. So I was more than a little surprised when I learned of the sheriff's office release to the press. Mr. Covey and I agreed with the sheriff's office that I would appear for arraignment at 9:00 A.M. on Wednesday, August 6.

To say that an arrest is preceded by—or at least followed by—an investigation is to state the obvious. But in this instance the sheriff's office chose to take exception to the rule. While their official report, which has remained confidential, mentioned nothing about assault, their release to the press and their arrest of me suggested that a rigorous examination of the evidence was in order. Nevertheless, they declined to question Bill Russell, the only witness to the accident; they did not check either car involved in the collision; and they made no effort to get in touch with or to question me. What they did do, contrary to the agreement we had made, was to arrest me on Tuesday night, nine hours before I was to be arraigned. The circumstances of the arrest involved a supremely odd set of coincidences. Although the sheriff's deputies were supposedly looking for me, they neither came to me nor called my house. Instead, they just happened to find me parked at midnight on San Vicente Blvd. I am rarely on that street and I was sitting in a car I had never been in before, and yet there in the darkness I was recognized by a passing deputy. Even more remarkably, that deputy was the same John Texeria who claimed that I had hit him during the incident involving Miss Chin.

I had been warned earlier in the day to beware of any such arrest and to accept it peacefully and without question, which I did. I was told that since the sheriff's office knew of the agreement the District Attorney had made to meet my lawyer and me, they were expecting me to argue and to resist, thus opening the possibility of retaliation on their part. What form that retaliation would have taken I leave you to decide.

Two addenda: The sequence of events leading to Eva Bohn-Chin's accidental fall from the balcony of Brown's apartment involved her residence in the United States on an expired passport. When the noise from the apartment drew two deputies to the door, battering, the girl was taken by panic, certain she would be asked for identification and aware of the likely consequences of deportation. She hid on the terrace, one floor above the courtyard below; then, frightened further by the struggle she heard inside—Brown trying to resist a complete search of the premises—she hung from the edge to avoid detection. That she should have reacted with such desperation and that she should have lost her grip and fallen, are propositions credible of themselves and overwhelmingly convincing in light of the ensuing refusal by the sheriff's office—despite Brown's requests—to produce either the signed document in which it claimed she had charged him with attempted murder or the document in which she professedly dropped the charge.

Also, Brown was persuaded that Texeira, upon the unexpected midnight apprehension and demand for immediate handcuffing and incarceration, hoped to provoke a blow, an expression of instinctive, unbridled rage, an act of violent resistance, which would justify him in shooting, killing Brown in self-defense. Indignation, fury, would be tempered by the general assumption that it was the predictable, if unfortunate, end toward which he had been heading ineluctably for years.

I complete the portrait now for the sake of balance and because it would seem to render the justification of Brown's claims finally undeniable. Even their inclusion, however, would not have saved the release from failure. As my friend Jeremy Larner, who had worked as Gene McCarthy's speechwriter, later told me: you've got to open a press release with a right-hand lead; you can't aim to write a literary essay, and you can't expect newspapers to emphasize points that you yourself wait for the end, obliquely, to make. Moreover, it would have ruined an institution. If one's first thought is that the Hollywood studios who look to make money from Brown's success in films and the liberal media who crusade for civil justice would have an interest in seeing the persecution terminated, further scrutiny might suggest precisely the contrary: that, in the first case, Brown's value as a salable property—particularly in the South, where his movies are in special demand—is not only undiminished but enhanced by a well-promoted image of force, cruelty, and recklessness; and that, in the second case, journalists will recognize better copy in spectacular charges and arrests than in complaints over mistreatment.

At any event, the coverage of the release was to the coverage of the accident and the arrest what the attention spent on a preseason scrimmage is to the attention spent on a Super Bowl. If it had been decided that the charges and nocturnal apprehension were worth lead-story infla-tion, the explanations and the counters were apparently of interest sufficient only to cramp them into a corner of page three. Beyond, nothing but sections explicitly posing an alternative account of the accident's details was included—not so much as a feint toward inference; silence on the false charges drawn up in the Eva Bohn-Chin case; no word of the curious ubiquity, the apparent extrasensory perceptions, of Texeira; no intimation that the sheriff's contract for the murder of Brown was the implicit allegation of the release. If I had come through for J.B. and for myself in effort, the gentlest comment one could submit about the execution was that it straddled the border of competence.

Paul Bloch and Richard Covey, Jim's lawyer, neither of whom had parried over the idea of an accusatory pretrial release in the first place, tried to discourage Jim from further pursuit. (Although Covey himself told the press, "Brown is the victim of a system that seems to make cannibals out of certain people.") But if one structures one's conception of oneself on the idea of self-reliance, if one insists upon serving as the harsh, self-appointed judge of one's actions and their consequences, then in all issues of more than passing concern, advice—no matter how noble the intention—becomes at best an irrelevance and at worst an annoyance. So after a preliminary hearing in which the (other appointed) judge remarked that although the charges seemed contradictory and weak, "even weak cases have to get sent on so the case will go to trial," Jim went ahead with his counterplot, pushing.

During a *Philbin's People* television program on which the other guests included Max Rafferty, Maureen Reagan, and Rudy Vallee, and for which the primary topic of discussion was to be sex education, Jim made it clear that he wanted to talk about his case. At the first opportunity, he opened up:

BROWN: All of you, I guess, live in California, and I've been trying to discover a way to live in California without having the Los Angeles sheriff's department on my back. And it seems that the last two years there has been a vendetta to bring me to my knees.

In this last situation I was accused by the sheriff's department in a release, a release to the national media which hit headlines all over the country, of first of all banging into the back of a pedestrian's car, then of refusing to give proper identification, and, finally, of driving my car at him to do him bodily harm—of pulling him off the hood of my car where he had—no, where they said I had hit him and he had landed and then grabbed the windshield wiper. It sounds like something out of Buck Rogers.

In actuality, none of this happened. The victim said that there was probably a mutual collision as he was pulling out into traffic and that my car was approaching. He then said that we both stopped and that I didn't give him information, and that as I was pulling away from the curb he felt that he had to stop me, so he jumped on the car. He claimed that although I was going five miles an hour, I was trying to run him over. He had a witness who said that when I stopped the car to take him off the hood, that I took him very gently and lifted him off the hood and then continued on my way.

Now my point is that there was a witness to this, the great basketball player Bill Russell, who was in my car. And this witness—the victim's witness—testified for me just as Russell would have. Now, before the charges were made—

PHILBIN: The second witness testified for you?

BROWN: Yes. He testified for me at the hearing—

PHILBIN: In your favor?

BROWN: Yes, in my favor. But before this there was no investigation whatsoever. Bill Russell was never approached to give his views on the accident. The cars were never checked. There was no damage on my car or on his car. I was never talked to. Four days later there were charges made on three counts—a felony and two misdemeanors. My attorney was called and said that we could come down that morning and meet these charges, but before that, that night, the night before at twelve o'clock, I was arrested by the same officer, Texeira, who had claimed about eight months ago that I had hit him.

Now, when the victim testified, all of the points that the sheriff's office had reported to the papers were totally different. So it led me to believe that Mr. Peter Pritchess, who is the head man of the sheriff's department, decided to bring me to my knees. He saw a great opportunity, and now I have to go through a trial to bring all of this out. And I think it's a ridiculous situation, because they did admit behind the scenes, after the judge called the D.A., that this case was absurd, that maybe they'd jumped the gun, because the sheriff's office would be a laughing stock, that they would be severely embarrassed, to say the least.

PHILBIN: A couple of questions: Why do you think the sheriff's department is having a *vendetta* against you, as you put it?

BROWN: Basically, there is an attitude in this country about manhood when it involves black people. I think I'm a person of integrity, and I tell the truth. I've always been a fighter, and I've always been controversial, because any black man in this country who speaks his mind on most issues becomes controversial.

I live in Hollywood in a manner in which I do things I like to do. I go out with people I like to go out with, white or black. I say what I want to say. And this is an attitude that some parts of America cannot stand. I am referred to as an arrogant nigger in certain quarters. Finally, Mr. Pritchess claimed that at some point I called him a bigot, a racist; although I've never met the man, this is the thing that's supposed to have been the immediate trigger for the vendetta. And I never have called him a racist. I've never even spoken to him, and that is the situation.

The hardest thrusts, however, were made privately. Brown acquired promises of support from the NAACP and CORE and passed around suggestions that there would be a concerted effort against Pritchess in his bid for reelection, at which point the sheriff began to withdraw. Apparently, the apprehension, the humiliation, of no one individual, no matter how personally distasteful or threatening to him, was worth his own general exposure as a charlatan, the loss of a position that carried power he would never achieve elsewhere. Acting from a role of weakness, he sent an emissary to Brown.

The choice was Chuck Connors, a film actor who had once played first base for the Dodgers. Connors was conceivably the only man alive who could claim warm relations and mutual respect with both Brown and Pritchess. If Jim liked his qualities of control and skill and toughness—qualities on a personal basis transcending any ideological considerations—Pritchess (a frustrated jock, a male sports groupie) was drawn to his athletic credentials and Reaganesque politics. The message conveyed took the form of an invitation to meet with Pritchess with an aim to clarifying and rectifying a most unfortunate matter, a regrettable *misunderstanding.*

Brown took his time, relishing the upper hand; at last agreed, and went to see his adversary. Pritchess suggested that the whole episode be ignored and forgotten. It was all a mistake. He had, of course, always admired Jim as a football star and never wanted any trouble with anyone, least of all with him. He could assure him that by accepting a simple traffic ticket (and also, by implication, by dropping all attempts to defeat him in his bid for reelection) the whole nasty issue would be closed. Sorry, said J.B., it had all been bullshit pure and plain and it was important from every angle that the trial go through so that the absurdity might be revealed for what it was, so that the string of arrests might finally be cut. Pritchess tried to hit the same hole from two or three other angles, couldn't, gave up, sadly, resigned himself to embarrassment.

The case of *The People of the State of California, Plaintiff, v. James Nathaniel Brown, Defendant,* in the Superior Court of the State of California for the County of Los Angeles, Hon. Charles H. Woodmansee, Judge, was dismissed in short order. The testimony of Arthur Charles Brush was rife with accusations so outrageous, so blatant in inconsistency and contradiction, as to create in the courtroom an atmosphere not so much of tension or anger as of bathos and farce; a testimony, moreover, whose absurdity was compounded physically in the figure of Brush—a massive, Mesozoic retrogression of the human form, close to three hundred pounds, malproportioned, walleyes peering through heavy lenses.

QUESTION BY MR. BALL (Brown's lawyer):
You leaped to the front of his car, didn't you? You leaped up on his car in some way or another? You vaulted onto his car?

ANSWER BY MR. BRUSH:
Yes, inasmuch as I'm capable of vaulting anything.

Q   You are not an athlete, are you?

A   No, sir.

Q   Not particularly agile at acrobatics?

A   No, sir.

Q   You can't do turns in the air, can you?

A   No.

Q   Well, when you leaped onto the car, did you fall on your stomach?

A   No.

Q When you leaped onto the car, what did you fall on?

A I didn't fall on anything.

Q What part of your body?

A My hip and buttocks.

Q Well, now, when you landed on Brown's car, you landed halfway back from the front end, didn't you?

A Yes.

Q Am I right?

A I would say so.

Q Halfway back?

A (Witness nods head up and down.)

Q Do you know how long that hood is?

A No.

Q Well, would you estimate the hood on Brown's car is eight feet from the front end to the windshield?

A No, I wouldn't make any estimate.

Q You'd make no estimate. Would you estimate that from the way you tell us this happened that you jumped four feet in the air?

A No.

Q Not that far? But you did land halfway back on the automobile?

A As I remember it, yes.

Q Now, furthermore, you demonstrated at the preliminary a vaulting—or Mr. Covey, the attorney for Mr. Brown at the preliminary examination demonstrated to you a suggestion as to how you got on the car, didn't he?

A Yes.

Q And he suggested that you got on there with your back to the driver and face forward for the way the automobile was going, didn't he?

A I don't remember that.

Q Well, let me read it to you...I will ask you if at the

time of the examination by Mr. Grodin, the deputy
district attorney, this question was asked of
you and if you didn't answer: "For the purpose of
the record, Mr. Covey demonstrated a vaulting
motion on the counsel table facing forward. Do I
understand you were facing forward in the motion of
the car? In other words, facing in the direction the car
was going? A: 'Yes.'" You so testified, didn't you?

A   Yes...

Q   At the preliminary examination you testified to the
Court the car started from the curb and turned to the
center, didn't you?

A   Yes.

Q   And you said that yesterday, didn't you?

A   Yes.

Q   And now did you tell us that the car turned out to the
center and then made a turn back toward your car?

A   Yes.

Q   That is right?

A   Yes.

Q   Is that by any chance because we have demonstrated
to you that the accident couldn't have happened that
way if it occurred as you testified yesterday?

A   No, sir.

The jury was unanimously and expeditiously convinced; the judge apologized to Brown, deemed the whole
proceeding a wasteful inconvenience; Brush, who had
sued for considerably more than a million dollars, left only
embarrassed; and the sheriff's department maintained its
perfect record of no convictions in its continuing series
of Jim Brown arrests. But it was, in an important sense, a
complicated, Pyrrhic victory, for although the probability
of future legal harassment had been diminished, the dis-

tortions would persist, and Brown would remain in large sectors of the American imagination a sadist and an animal, and, perhaps for that very reason, would also remain in such sectors irresistibly appealing, a star.

Airport

Several weeks later, back in New York, I spoke to Jim on the phone, learned he would be flying to Spain, making a late-night connection at Kennedy Airport. I agreed to meet him, spend an hour between flights, see him off. I went to Elaine's for dinner, found my friend Jack Richardson, the critic and dramatist, sitting with a group of writers, and joined him. Gay Talese, A. E. Hotchner, Bob Wool, David Halberstam. It is hard to feel uncomfortable with Jack around, one of the smartest, quickest, most congenial men I know. And Wool and Talese were fine, if infrequent, eating companions. But the projection from Halberstam, awkward, heavy, dour, was oppressive.

One had begun admiring Halberstam, his early Vietnamese dispatches, his eloquent and not ineffectual protestations; and he had written a hilarious devastation of Ted Sorensen and the politics of sycophancy. But then, startlingly, in *McCall's*, he had written "Farewell to the 60s," an insufferably windy lamentation that contained what was conceivably the most mean-spirited, pathetic passage ever to appear in an essay aspiring to seriousness:

I remember with a certain amount of pleasure a small incident from the summer of 1969: an island off Maine, friends bring up a young Negro literary figure, very bright, very attractive, and he knows this full well, he's the only one on the island, and he plays it for all it's worth. Well, you can't blame him, he's waited a long time for this; but in every gesture and every word is the assumption that he has soul and we do not.

But on the second night an old friend of mine, who is a writer and a musician, takes him out to find something to drink, and they return about 1:00 A.M. with two small musical instruments, and as they re-enter the party, my friend turns and says, "Hey, man, let's take off all our clothes and go jaybird naked playing these instruments." And the Negro won't do it—he's too uptight. And I have a feeling, God bless my friend, that he scored one for our side; he outsouled them.

The contest for "soul" is to important racial competition what canasta is to a championship prize fight. And Halberstam won't even play the canasta himself; will choose instead the vicarious thrill of watching his friend sit in. The bitterness, the envy, the anxiety, the hatred, speak of a fear so debilitating as to render inconceivable any relation of mutual honesty or respect with a black man of even the most elementary pride. That most white Americans will read the passage with a grateful sense of identification serves to indicate precisely how desperate the situation has become.

Halberstam was controlling the conversation, concocting a list of ten worst-dressed men in New York, drawing nominations from Hotchner and Talese. I started a sideshow with Jack, mentioned I would be going to see Jim after dinner. Someone overheard, wondered whom Jim had tossed out of his window lately. No doubt I should have ignored it, should have understood that protestations, explanations, would be fruitless. But I didn't; succumbed instead to the sense of impatience and anger the remark had engendered. Worse, I tried to be polite, couching the justification, the long rendition of the sheriff's vendetta, in the tone and language of apology.

Having been so established in the role of arbiter, Halberstam was only too happy finally to conclude that he "couldn't buy it"; the man had a bad chip on his shoulder and that was all there was to it; Brown was hostile, arrogant.

"Oh, then you know him also," I said.

"Well, not personally," said D.H. "But I know him

from what I've heard from people who do. I get the same view from all of them."

"Who are they?"

"Different people."

"Which ones?"

"Well (his patience was being taxed, his voice taking on an edge), I've read several articles."

"Whose?"

"Gloria Steinem's for one. I don't remember the others."

"Gloria Steinem is a good friend of Jim's," I said. "Besides, the article you're referring to is the most flattering. There's not a word in it that suggests anything about chipped shoulders."

Halberstam shrugged—bored, unconvinced. He couldn't be wrong; because if he was, he would have to rethink his line, shake the sweet neatness of his respectable neo-racism. He might even have to assume that his old friend, the writer and musician, couldn't "outsoul" Brown; and if *he* couldn't, who, in the name of Wayne Cochran, could?

I left, frustrated and angry largely at myself for wasted persistence.

I arrived early at the TWA building in Kennedy, wandered around the domed lobby, waited. When at last I found him, his back was turned and he didn't see me. He was standing with two men and their wives, all in early middle age, the men immaculately groomed with short hair, thin ties, heavy-soled shoes; the women sturdy, fresh, blissfully out of style. The four were laughing, half-bowing at Brown, shaking his hand, eliciting autographs. He—smiling, nodding, signing—looked happy, relaxed; swaying slightly, rhythmically, side to side, black silk t-shirt and navy bells. And suddenly I had a flash, a crystalized moment of recall, in which I became aware of what it was that had kept, would keep, me close to Brown, of what concrete and actual qualities had gradually transformed the mythical, fantastic conception I had held and been drawn to in the beginning.

The clothes were not simply tailored well, colored subtly, as always, but, more, recalled and suggested muted, refined, quiet taste, characteristic to the point of self-definition. Never a dull story or joke, never an obtrusion or ignorant opinion, never a cowardly lie. No clumsiness of movement, no grossness of gesture, no bullying demonstrations of force. No gratuitous slights, no timid evasions, no greedy impositions of need.

"Hey!"

"Toe!"

Extricated, he came over, radiant; I couldn't remember ever having seen him so happy. We went up a spiral staircase to the London Club, sat at the bar.

"There's *something*. I can see that."

Jim smiled. "Can you really?"

"Absolutely. What is it?"

"It's weird." He started laughing, quietly, looking away, embarrassed. I waited. "I met this girl, Toe. It's weird."

"What girl? You in love or something?"

The words out, I knew that that was what it had to be.

"She's the singer from The Friends. Jesse. It's wild, Toe. I've never had anything like it. It's as if over the past month or so we've come to reach this fantastic understanding and feeling for each other. A completely straight thing. I mean there's no way in the world either of us could be untruthful. I know her needs and she knows mine, and we respect them and accept them and act with them in mind. So there's no shame or guilt or game-playing or role-maneuvering or any other kind of shit. She knows what I feel, I know what she feels, and whatever might happen when we're on our own, it's okay, because we know that as soon as we're back together everything is going to be laid right out and the closeness will be strong."

I was surprised at first, couldn't see him as vulnerable in the present, although he had told me he had felt so at times in the past; but then I understood that it wasn't vulnerability at all, but rather, simply, an unqualified openness, presenting the same possibilities with few of the dangers and which, further, was available only to someone whose sense of himself, of his own reliability and power, was sure before the union began.

"And you know, even though I'm aware that some cats seeing her from the outside wouldn't see any physical beauty in her I find her beautiful myself. No one like her in the world. It's a feeling her presence brings, that everything's all right. I can go anywhere, do anything, deal with any shit I have to and *laugh* through it because I know I have her to come back to."

Reduced to monosyllables I could utter only: "Wow... that's...wow." Enlarged, too, for I knew, even while listening to him, a vague, wonderful sensation, a recollection, a projection of the same yearning in myself, a longing for that very condition.

"What's up with you, Toe? How's your work going?" The voice was tighter now, the look into my eye; the shyness, self-exposure, back in control.

"Well, I have a proposition. The *Esquire* thing isn't going to work out and I don't think that what I want to do can be holed up in an article anyway. I want to do a book."

If the idea had occurred to me at all before that moment, it had been neither developed nor formed. Improvising, I followed my lead.

"A book about everything that's happened between us; a book, really, about the effect you've had on me and what implications flow from it."

The thought seized me as I spoke that J.B. would be sour on it, master, Mr. C., *using* once again; spook, slave, cashing in on his labor. Exploit it, it's yours.

"Sounds fine, Toe."

"No hesitations?"

"No. Look, it goes without saying I trust you; I know that whatever you put in will be true. But even if you were someone else and I didn't trust you, even if the cat had a thing against me and were out to lie and make me look bad, what kind of weak sucker would I be if I couldn't handle it? I know who I am and what I do, so it doesn't really matter. I'll be looking to read it, big Toe; even expect to learn some new stuff about myself..."

He started chuckling.

"Hey, but I'll tell you, boy! Sure as hell can't see it being any more about me than it is about you!"

Waiting for a boarding announcement, we talked, further, oddly, uncharacteristically, mainly about football. He spoke with care, hesitating, as though here, in apparently the most public part of himself, he felt most guarded, private.

"I always used to *watch*, Toe. I was always looking to learn new ways of doing things. And it's strange, because sometimes I discovered the most important stuff from the most unlikely sources. I never really knew how to make sure I could score from inside the one until I studied Don Bossler. But when I caught what he was doing, I had it down for good myself. Instead of making your move first, see, you wait for a split second for the line to make its move: if it comes in at you high—*boom!*—you drive through low; if it comes at you down—*shoot!*—you leap in high. It's that simple, but very few running backs know it or follow it.

"And then there's the whole question of learning how to run. People used to watch a classic case like Hugh McElhenny and assume that because he was such a beautiful gazelle, everyone should try to run the same way: head down, *high stepping.* But apart from a few extraordinary exceptions, it's unnatural; just the opposite is what should be taught. Also, they tell you to run with the ball tucked in. That's absurd. It slows you down and it limits your agility. You should *cover* the ball, but with your hand and forearm, so you can run in your rhythm, free.

"Did you ever think about the philosophy of exercise? Coaches have the idea that certain standard programs of conditioning are good and have to be valid for everyone who's trying to get in shape. But think about it. A man who's paid to run needs to use different muscles, be in a different kind of shape, from a man who's paid to block or from a man who's paid to kick or throw. The exercises should reflect the function; sharpen each player physically along the lines of his own needs and in relation to the services he's relied on to perform."

"You're going to convince me you want to be a coach," I said.

"Shit, no!" Jim said, laughing. "That part of my life is over. I don't go back."

The announcement came; we walked down the stairs, through the lobby and the long red and white corridor leading to the departure gates, Jim signing as he walked for several who moved with us, sideways, by him, off their own routes but gladly along, awed, white and black, all.

It was into the morning, and the circular embarkation area, low florescent acoustical ceiling with random pattern, hard white-tile floor, was empty except for the passengers leaving on Jim's flight to Madrid. One man, a large, thickly built army private with red hair shaved butch; a bridgeless nose; thin, short lips; ruddy, blotched skin; small, yellow eyes, stood slightly off to the side, away from the others, staring at us. I don't think Jim noticed him, but I had been intrigued, wondering at the stiff, hard pose he was striking, as though waiting for his sergeant to order him at ease. Jim extended his hand and I shook it. I wished good luck, said I looked to hear from him soon, to see him.

"Good-bye, brother," he said, and walked away and disappeared onto the ramp.

"Brother," says Locke, "is the name of friendship and equality, and not of jurisdiction and authority."

There, finally. Said. Through the only hole I, a white man in America, could ever have entered. *Brother*. From filial to fraternal; taking to sharing. *Brother*.

I turned to the line of phones on the wall behind me, made two calls to arrange the hours ahead. It was several minutes into the second call that I sensed, *knew*, that the army private, forgotten, was still standing in the same place, staring, alone now, hateful. But this time I was not curious, not intrigued. Just afraid. For if he was, in fact, there, I would have to face him and deal with whatever it was he wanted of me; and incredibly, after all the distance I thought I had moved from the time I had met Jim, after all I believed I had learned, I doubted seriously that I could. I hung up, turned, found him, expression unaltered, there.

I wanted to run; even pushed off my left foot, just enough to give away the intention, and then jammed back on the right, held. It would have required no great effort of ingenuity or speed to escape. There were several exits available nearby, and through one of them I could see an attendant at the other end of the corridor. Or I could have yelled and drawn immediate assistance. But such possibilities of flight exist, finally, only in fantasy, for they lead never to safety, but to deeper emptiness and to greater fear. So I stood trembling, forcing slow, deep breaths to counter the frantic pounding of my heart, and watched him walk toward me. He stopped no more than a foot away, relaxed now, leaning slightly forward, larger, thicker even, than I had thought.

"That was James Brown you were with, wasn't it?" His voice was peculiarly hollow, high in pitch, an aggressive drawl. The eyes narrowed into something close to slits, vanishing, so that I became aware now only of his body, heavy arms, his loud, hard breath. (Loud and quick. Was it possible he, too, was frightened? As frightened as I was?)

"That's right."

"What are you," he said, jerking his head at me, "some kind of a actor?"

"No."

"Well, you ain't no football player. What are you, his representative or something?"

"No."

"Well, what are you then?"

"I'm his friend." If even a remote possibility of running had remained, it was now gone.

"His *friend!*" The eyes opened again and I glared into them; but my legs were light to the point of weightlessness, and a soft shove would in all likelihood have sent me down. "You're his *friend*?" He snorted. If indeed he was afraid, he was doing a masterful job of masking it. "Ain't that some shit! Now you tell me, boy, you tell me: What is James Brown? He ain't nothin' but another *nigger*, ain't that right?"

He edged an inch closer, and for the first time I was conscious of the alcoholic reek in his breath. I had no idea what to say; couldn't have spoken if I had, the churning in my stomach by now far too severe.

"I asked you a question, boy. I said James Brown's just another black-ass nigger like the rest of them. Is that right or are you callin' me a liar?"

Somehow, I tightened; suspended respiration, stiffened my gut. I trained my eye on the left side of his jaw, my right arm loose, and suddenly, shot up through it, fist closing, hard, nails pressing into my palm. I heard a thump, a loud break, and saw him stumble backward, stunned, balance gone, on his way down. But before he had fallen all the way, I jumped forward and swung again, striking him in the same spot, crashing him flat on the tile, his head landing, bouncing twice on the floor. I watched the blood start to drip, flow freely from his mouth, and I stood over him, shaking more violently even than before, exhilarated, released. Groaning, the soldier rolled over on his side. I turned and walked away, through the white corridor with the red carpet, into the almost empty lobby and then outside, cracked wide open.

PUBLISHED BY RAT PRESS
RP003
FIRST EDITION OF 3000 PRINTED IN 2009
ISBN 978-0-9818056-3-4

COVER PHOTOS: ALEX GOTFRYD, LYNNE GORDON,
AND HENRY GROSKINSKY

PRINTED IN CANADA

DESIGN: FREE ASSOCIATION
WWW.FREE-ASSOCIATION.ORG

WWW.RATPRESS.COM